Powell's   I Know You're Somewhere (NoDJ)

PC

Art & Graphic Design   102649

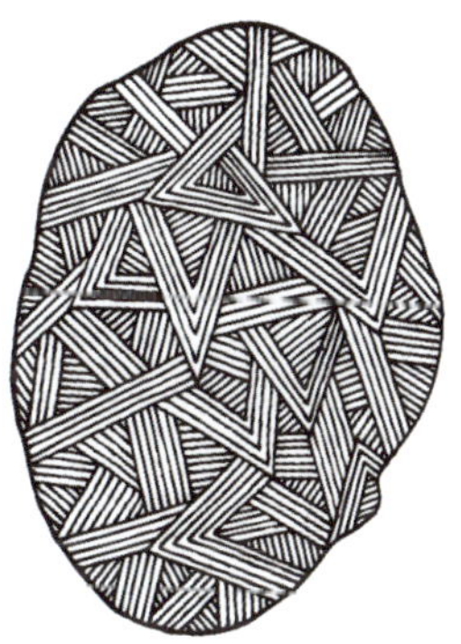

IAN JOHNSON | I KNOW YOU'RE SOMEWHERE

KIND OF BLUE

**"I hear a note by one of the fellows in the band and it's one color.
I hear the same note played by someone else and it's a different color.
When I hear sustained musical tones, I see just about the same colors
that you do, but I see them in textures. If Harry Carney is playing, D is
dark blue burlap. If Johnny Hodges is playing,
G becomes light blue satin."**

- Edward Kennedy "Duke" Ellington, composer, pianist, bandleader (1899-1974)

San Francisco based artist Ian Johnson is well known for creating detailed realistic portraits of canonical American jazz musicians positioned within abstract geometric compositions of space and color. Over the past several years, he has adeptly activated elements of graphic design to create visually seductive environments of rhythm, depth, and texture that undergird portraits of individuals indispensible to America's cultural heritage - Louis Armstrong, Miles Davis, Duke Ellington, Billie Holiday, Dave Brubeck, Thelonious Monk, Abbey Lincoln, John Coltrane, Ornette Coleman.

There's a lot more going on here, however, than portraiture and composition in Johnson's paintings and drawings on paper and wood panel. Bringing into play the perspective of science, Johnson's work can be viewed and understood differently through the lens of synesthesia, a psychosomatic condition in which one type of sensory stimulation evokes the sensation of another, such as when hearing a sound produces a visualization of color. This book, consisting of Johnson's most recent body of work, is a broad collection that invites the viewer to not just look, but also to listen, to the images.

The history of the physiological and psychological bases of sound advanced rapidly during and after the Scientific Revolution of the 17th Century. Galileo Galilei, Marin Mersenne, and others built upon observations of acoustic phenomena by the ancient Greek philosopher Pythagoras some 2,000 years earlier, creating a deeper understanding of how sound is transmitted and eventually perceived. Galileo wrote, "Waves are produced by the vibrations of a sonorous body, which spread through the air, bringing to the tympanum of the ear a stimulus which the mind interprets as sound." Speech, music, laughter, thunder, sirens, creaks, engine noises - all forms of sound function as a result of the same fundamental scientific principle, namely that of physical vibrations travelling from a point of origin through space and time to the vicinity of our ears. These vibrations enter our body through the ears, where they are transduced into nerve impulses that proceed to the brain in order to be ultimately perceived as sound.

There is an awe-inducing beauty to this process as it relates to music. The construction of melody, rhythm, harmony, and cadence in a musician's mind manifests into both notes laid down on a score and physical interaction with instruments to animate these ideas into concrete physical vibrations that traverse space and transform into music in our heads. While musicians use countless unique methods to compose their music, imagine - as the great Duke Ellington states

"I can see forms and shapes in my mind when I solo, just as a painter can see forms and shapes when he starts a painting. And I can see different colors. My cymbals will be one color and my snare another color and my tom-toms each a different color. I mix these colors up, making constant movement. Drums suggest movement, a conscious, constant shifting of sounds and levels of sound. My drumming can shade from a whisper to a thunder."

- Elvin Jones, drummer, bandleader (1927-2004)

"When I hear sustained musical tones, I see just about the same colors that you do, but I see them in textures" - compositions being written by sequences of color and texture rather than chord progressions. Two of Johnson's works on paper, Black Fire (pg. 28) and Complete Communion (pg. 29), tangibly illustrate this idea, where musicians Andrew Hill, Don Cherry, and Henry Grimes are holding sheet music consisting not of notes, but rather of units of shape and color. Music existing as visual stimuli.

Many of these musicians composed and recorded seminal works in the 40s, 50s and 60s, leaving behind a musical legacy that resonates decades later. Johnson's use of color, line, and abstract design mirrors this era of musical innovation. As Johnson states, "I like having black and white portraits representing the artists in the past as they were, and then having colors and patterns represent the music carrying on and being alive now." The moment of creative transmission still exists as soon as the music hits our ears, even with songs written, performed, and recorded over 50 years ago. In Spirits Rejoice (pg. 26), Johnson pictures saxophonist Albert Ayler and his younger brother Donald on trumpet with lines of color radiating from each musician's head, intersecting, overlapping, and vibrating in proximity to each other. The lines fill the entire composition,

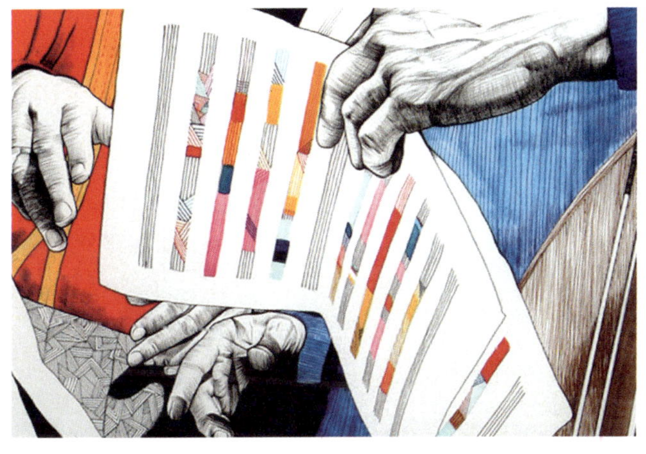

falling off the page. One can imagine these lines, like Elvin Jones states, as "movement, a conscious, constant shifting of sounds and levels of sound." Visual stimuli existing as music.

Enjoy digging into this book. In addition to appreciating Johnson's artistic prowess, compositional balance, and genuine reverence for the musicians portrayed, I hope you can also hear the work - the keening skeletal melodies of Ornette Coleman, the propulsive rhythms of Art Blakey, the emotional and free yet classically structured sound of Eric Dolphy.

Kevin B. Chen

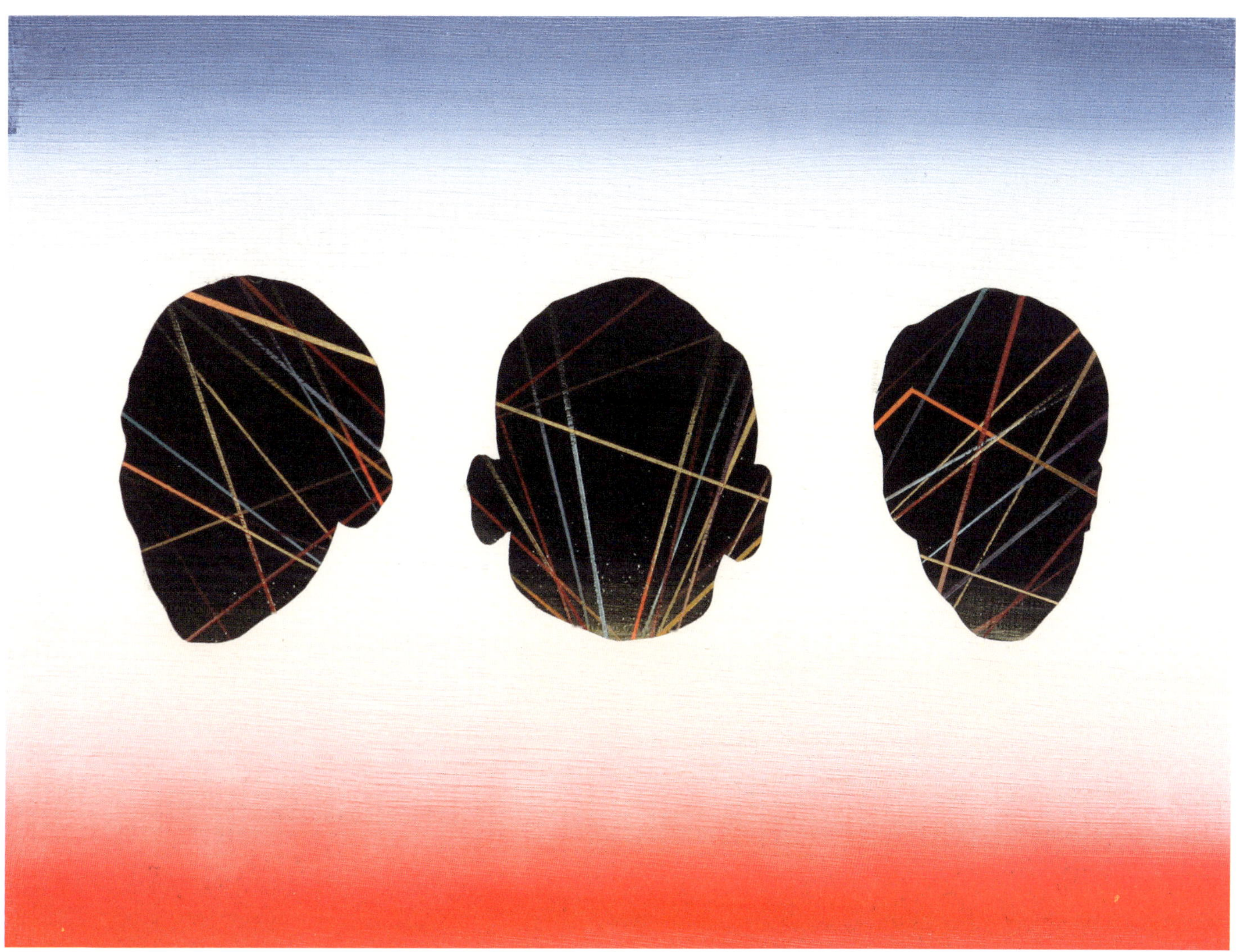

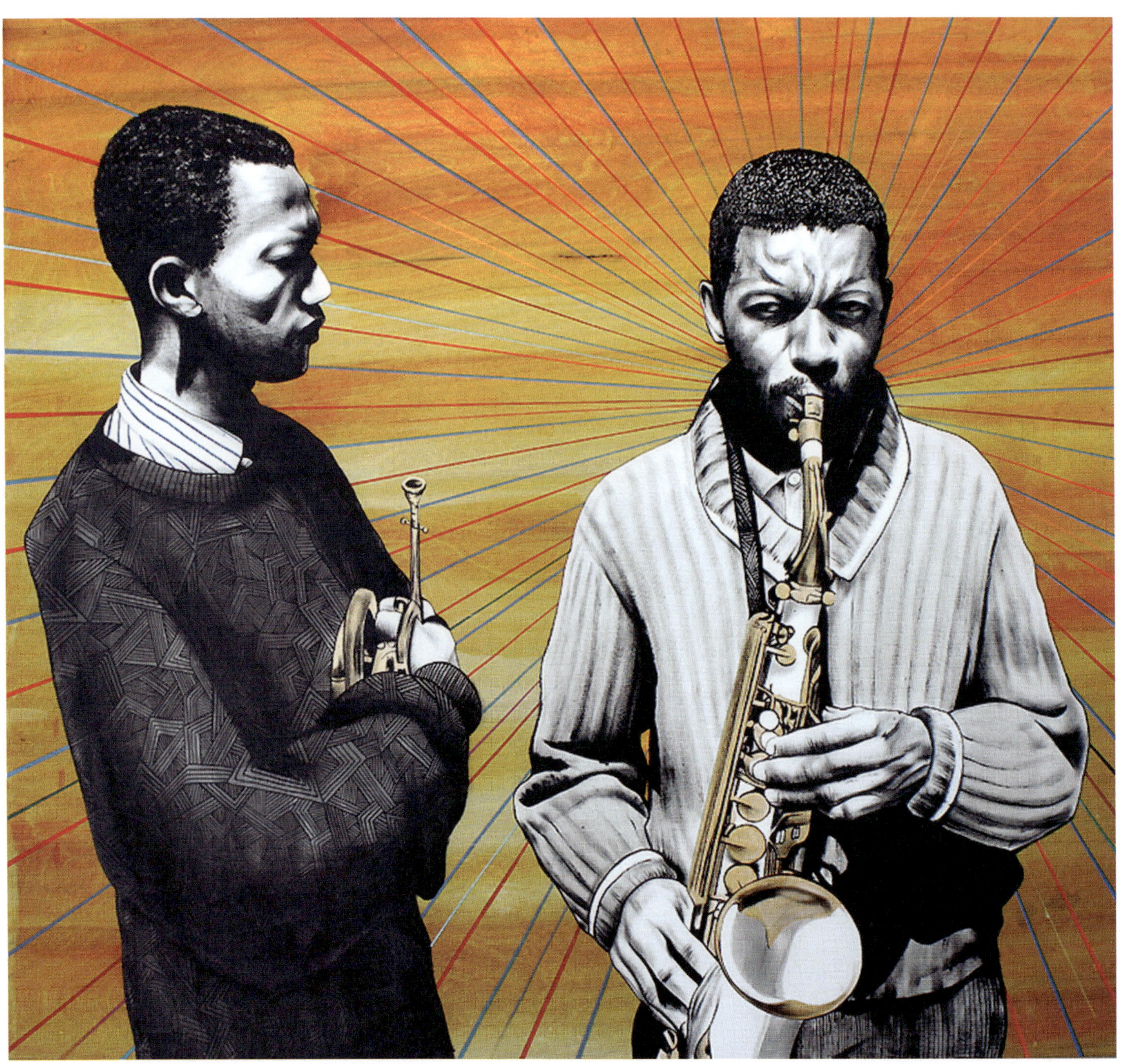

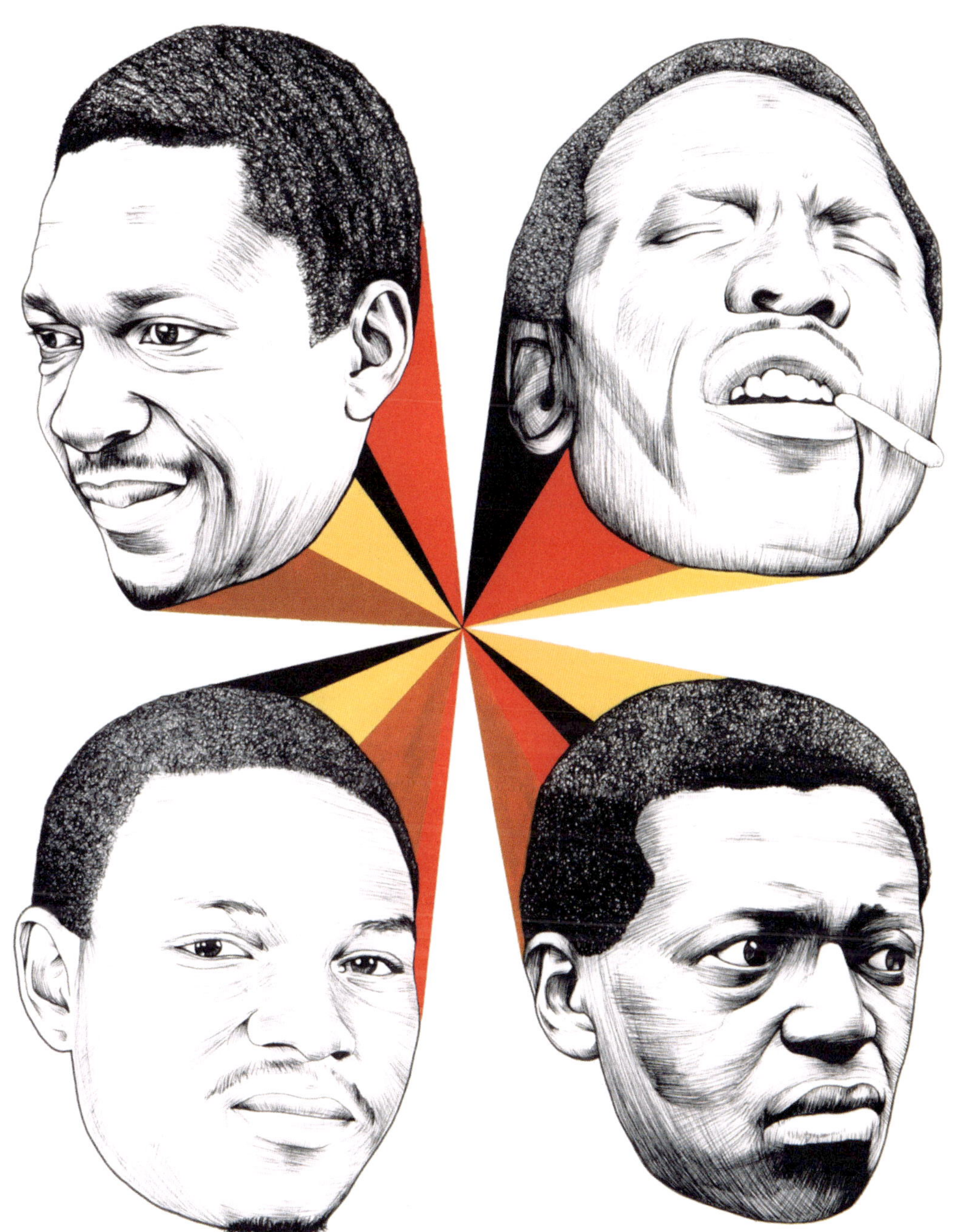

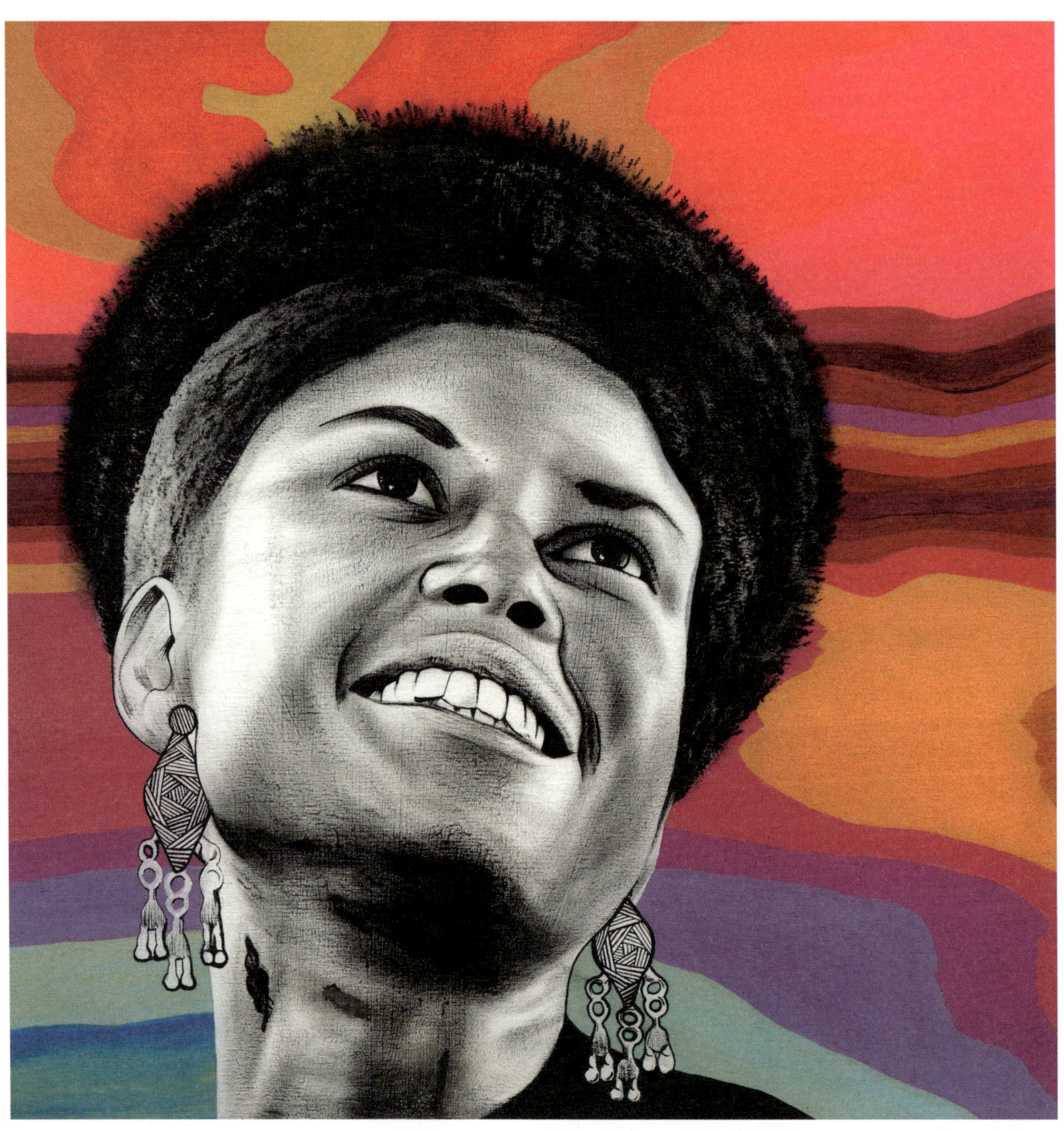

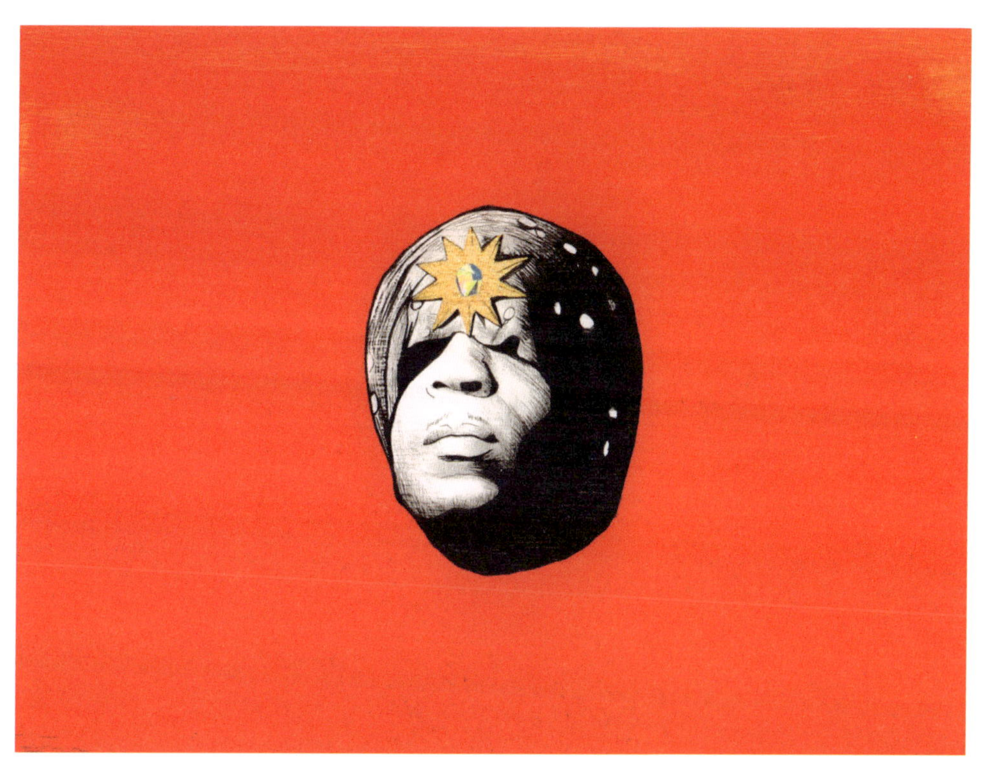

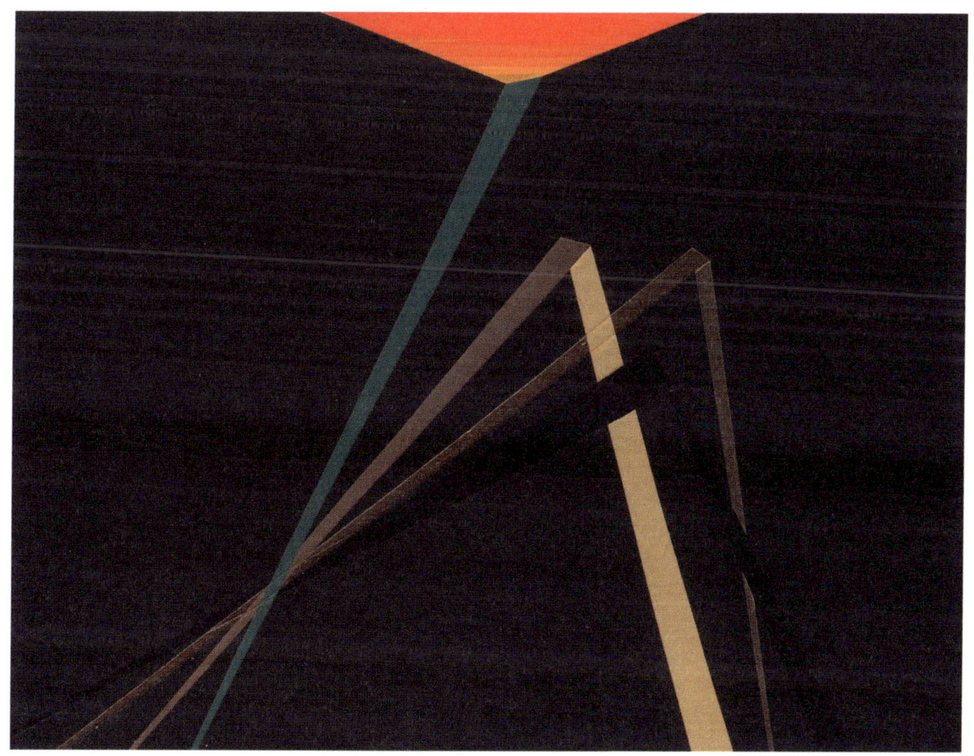

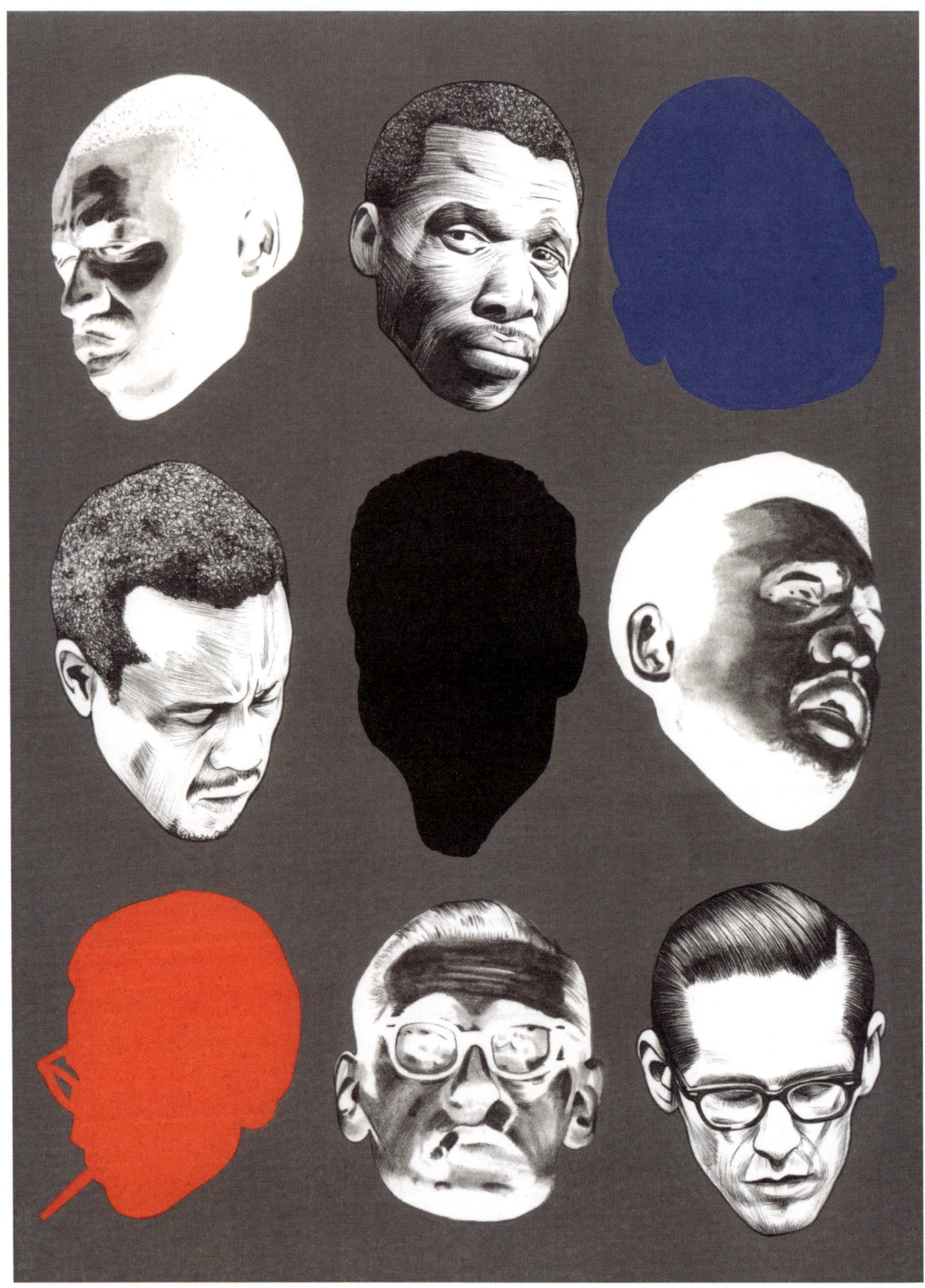

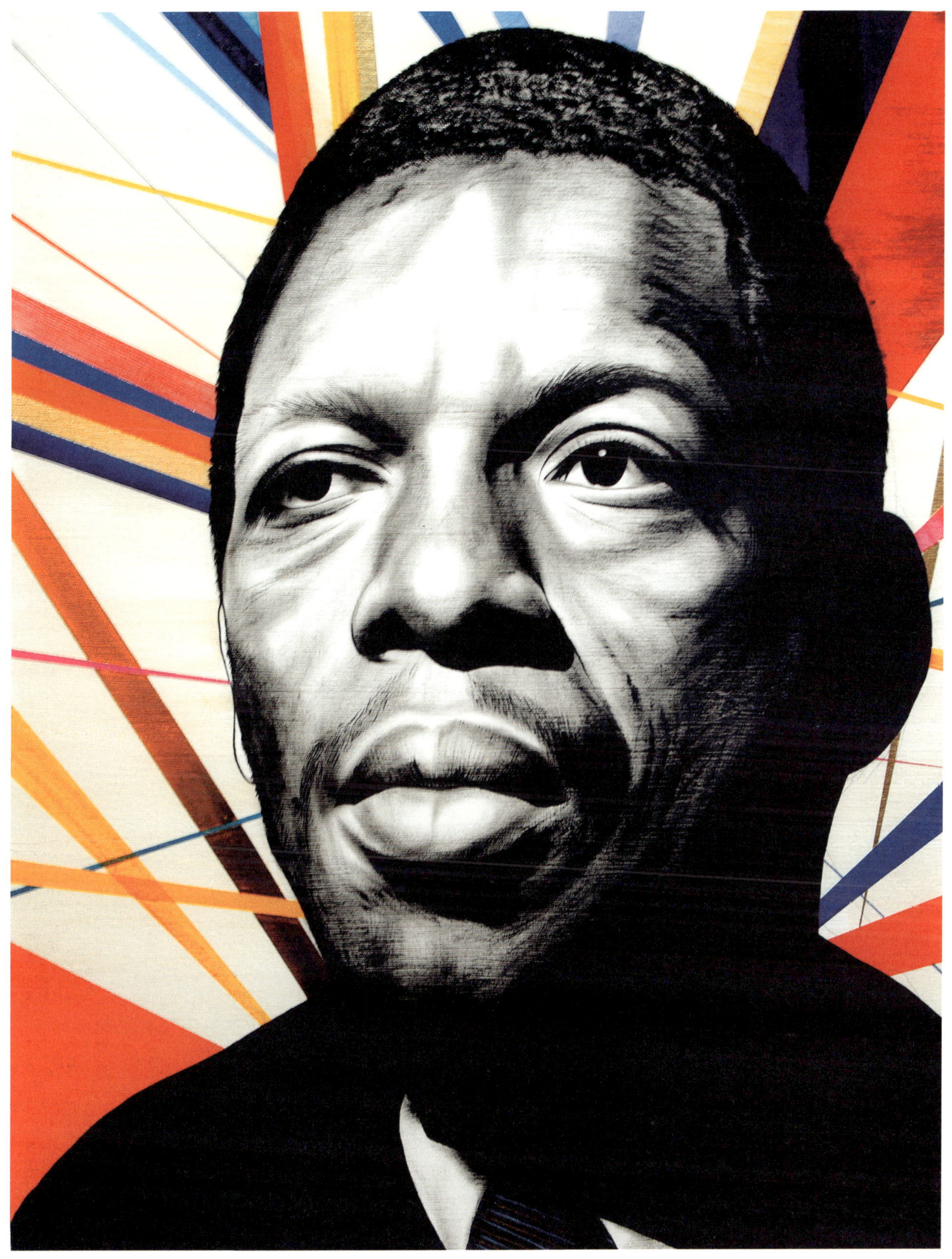

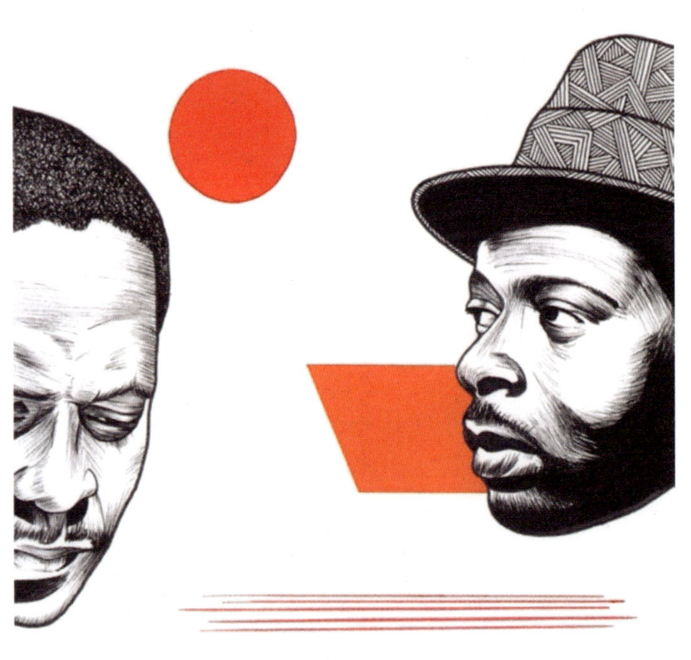
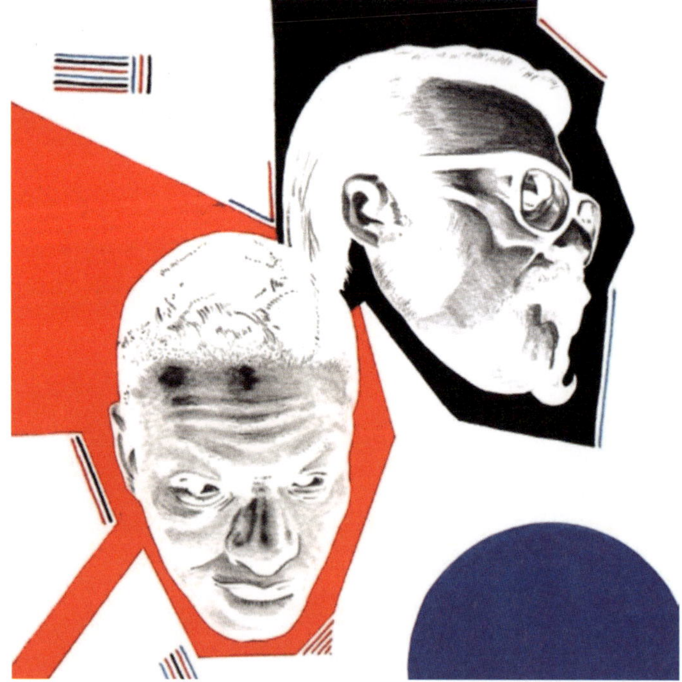
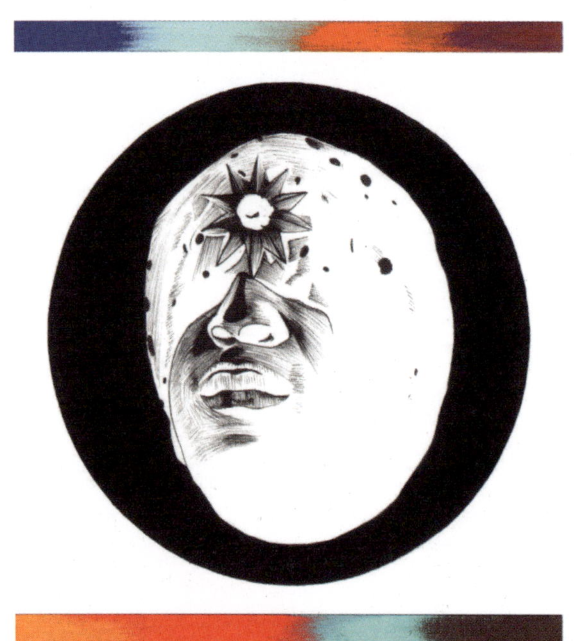
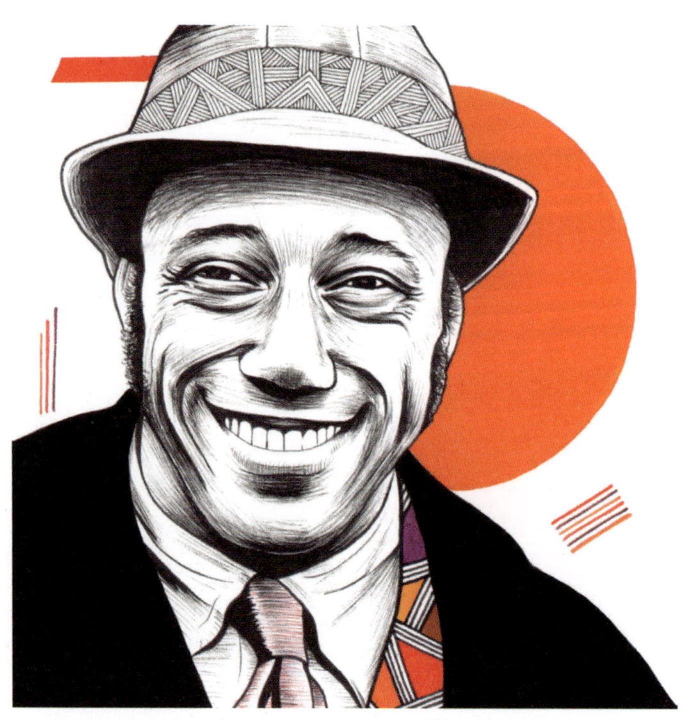

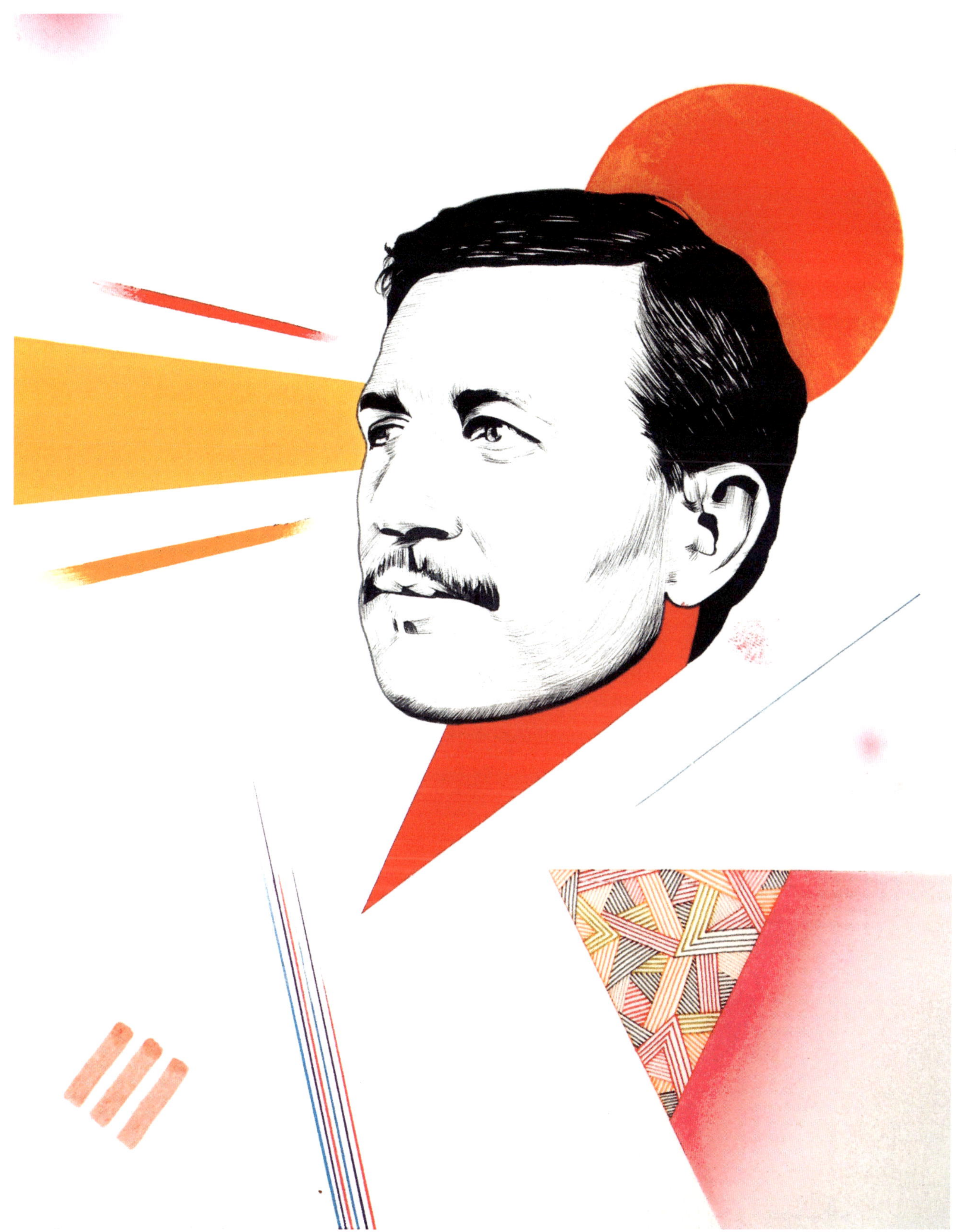

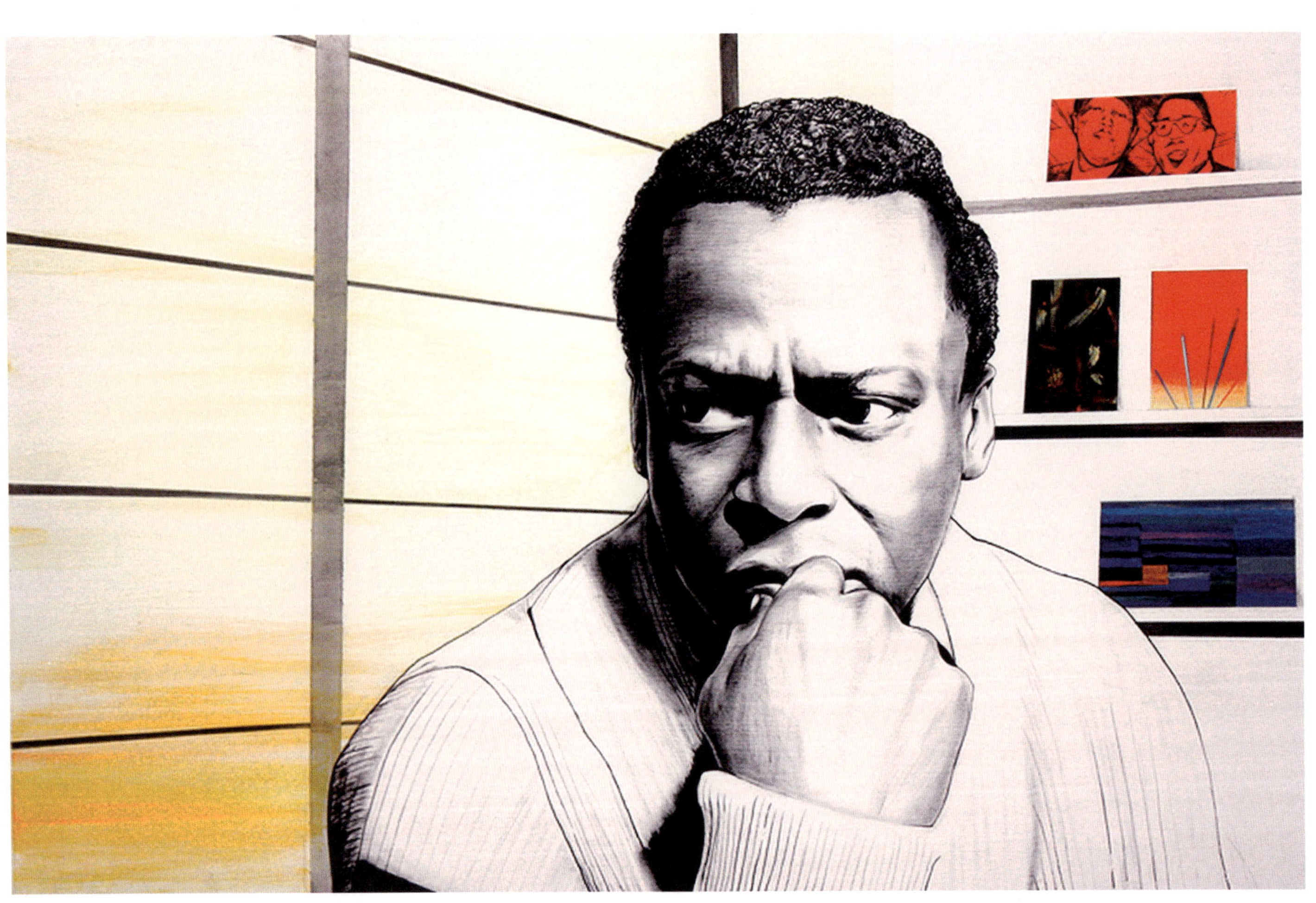

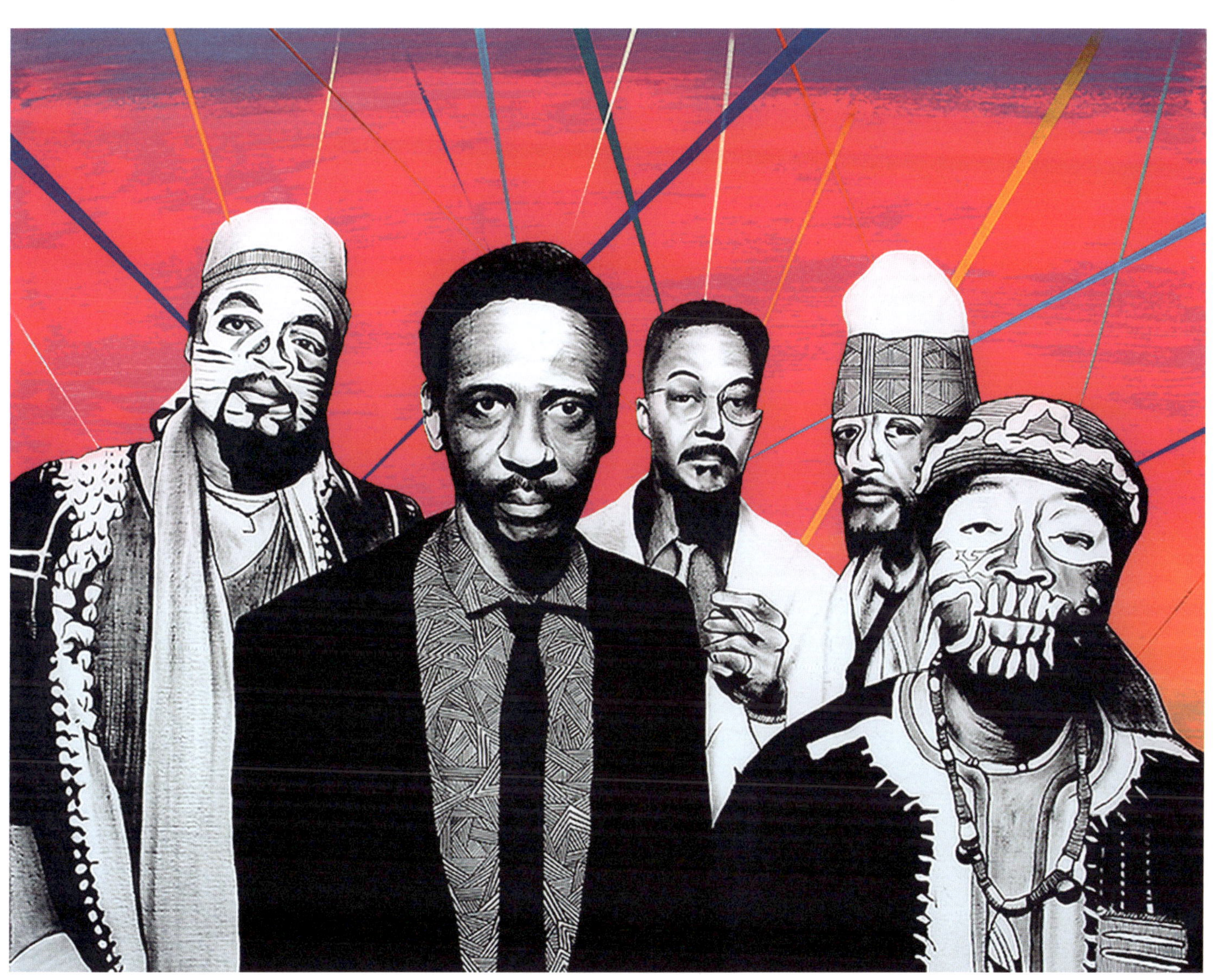

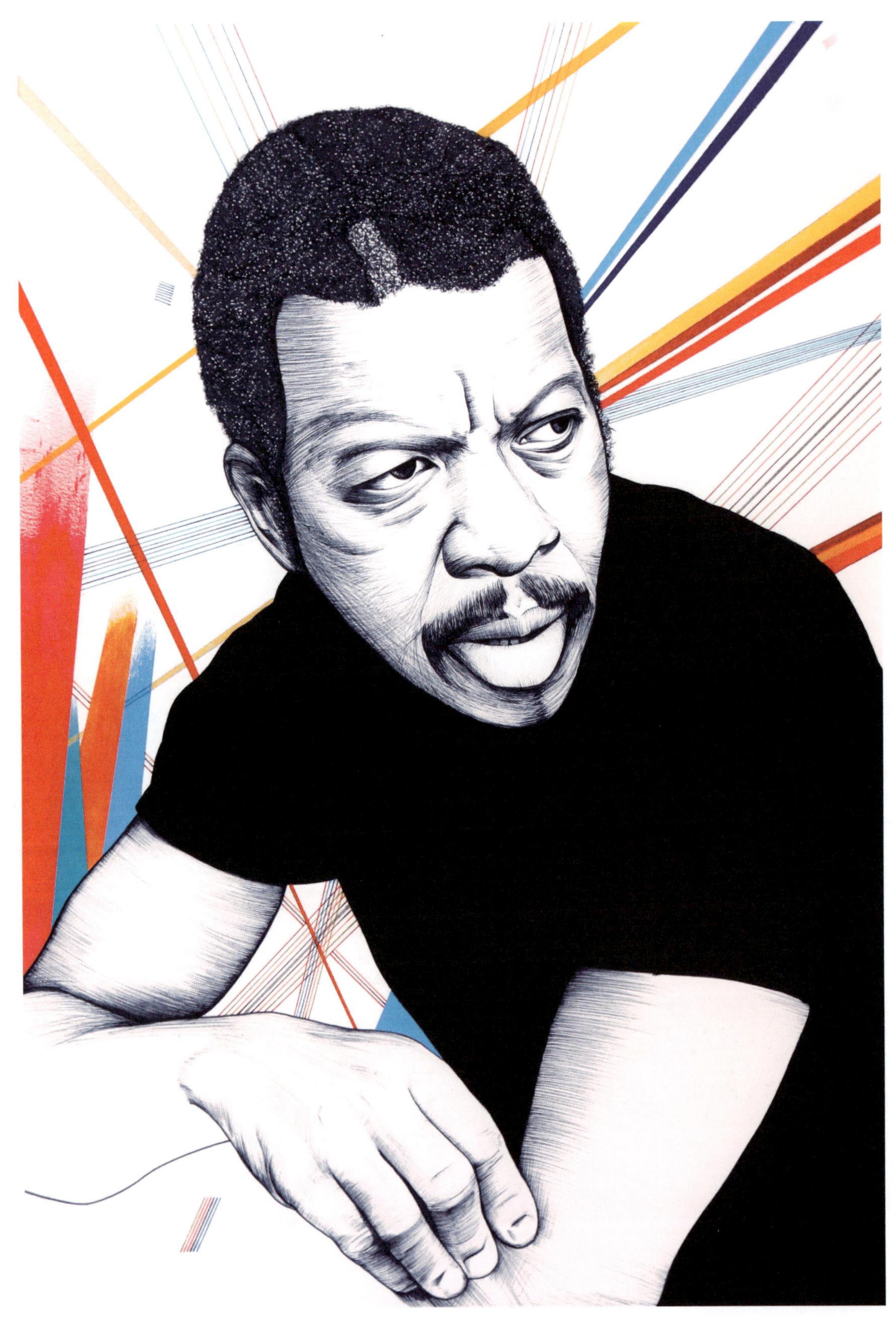

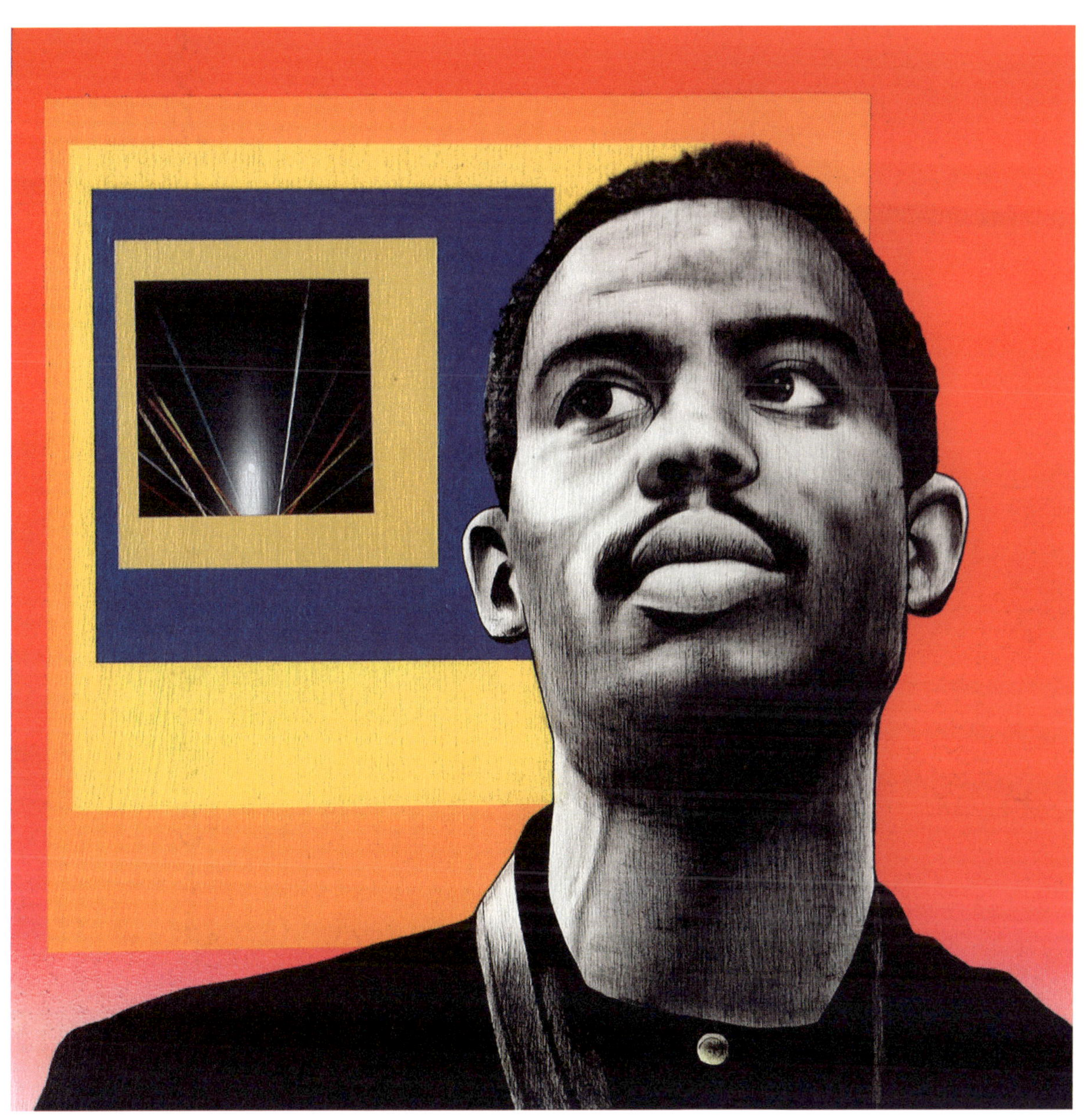

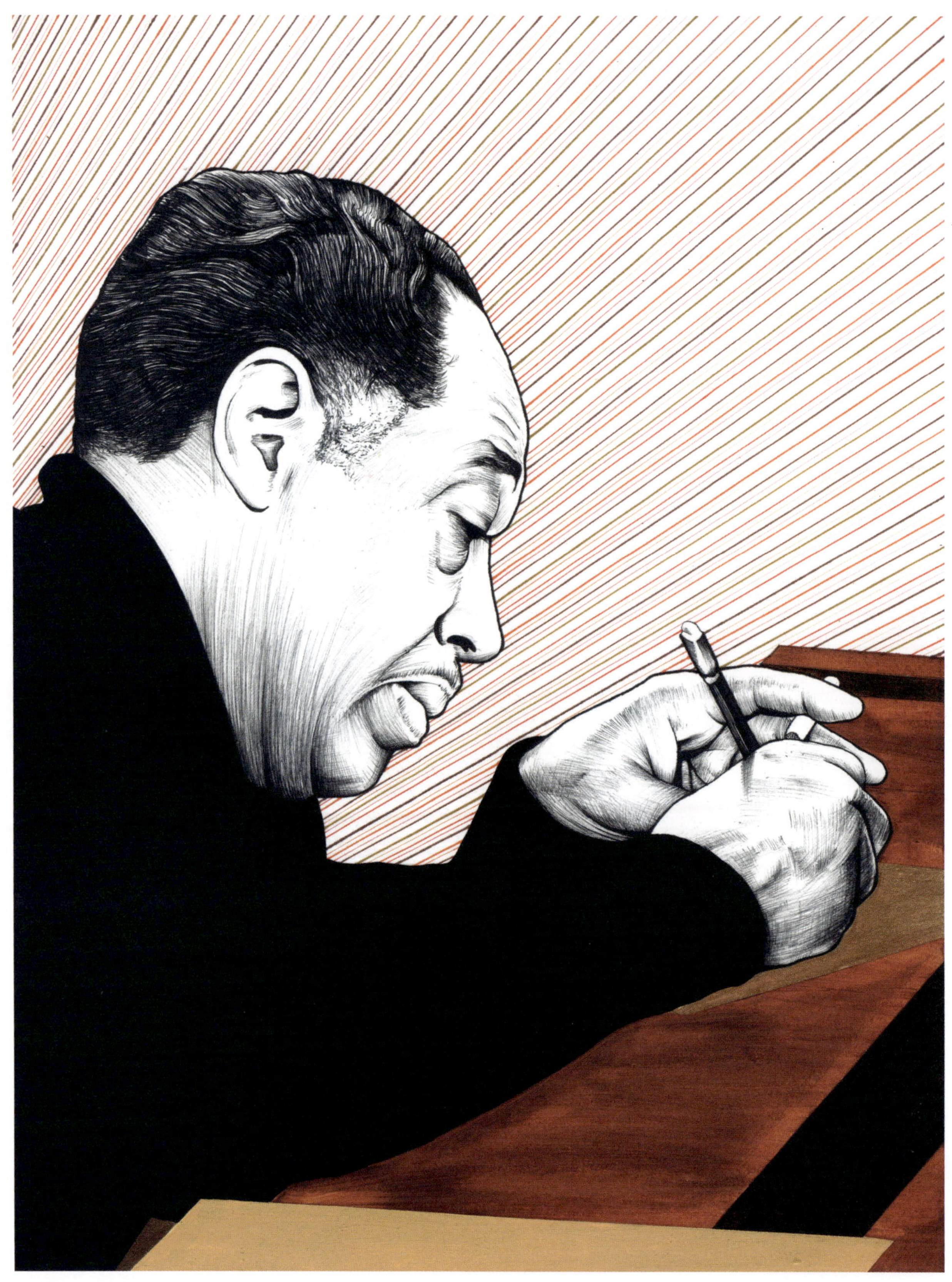

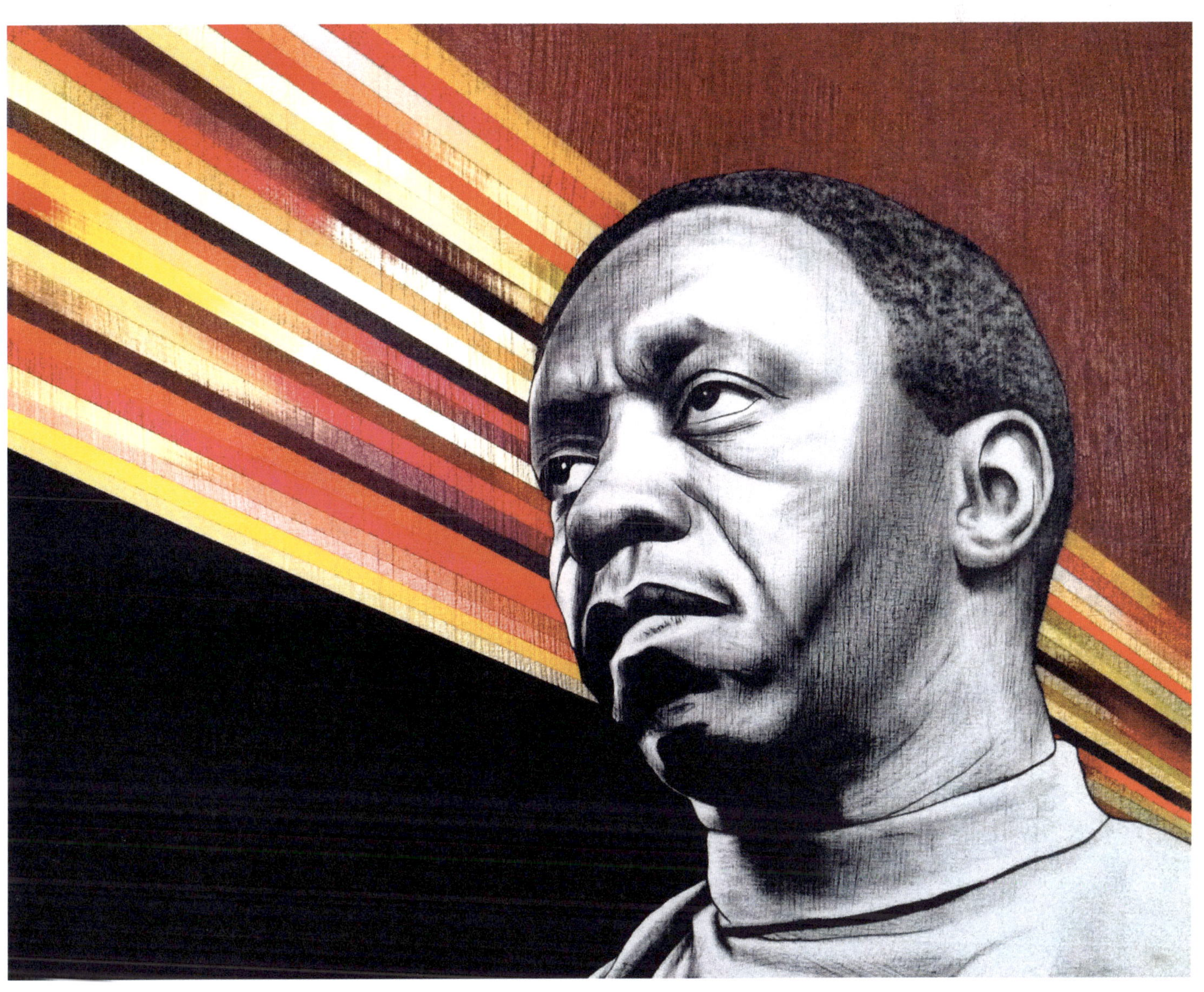

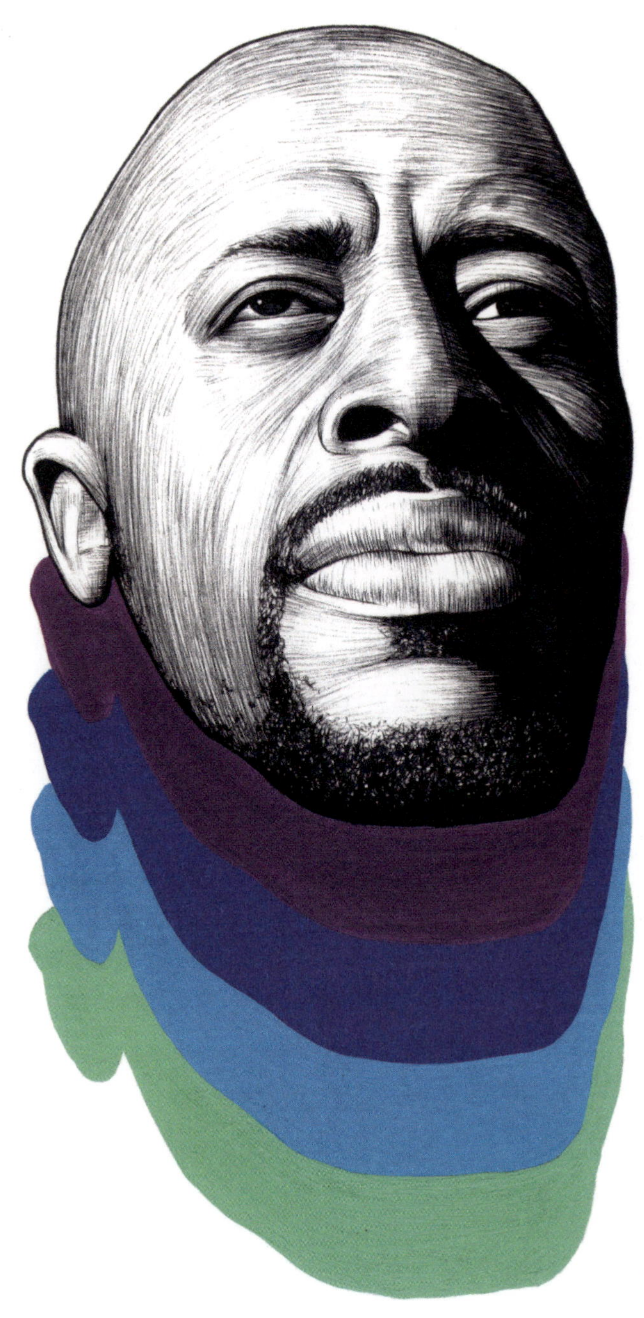

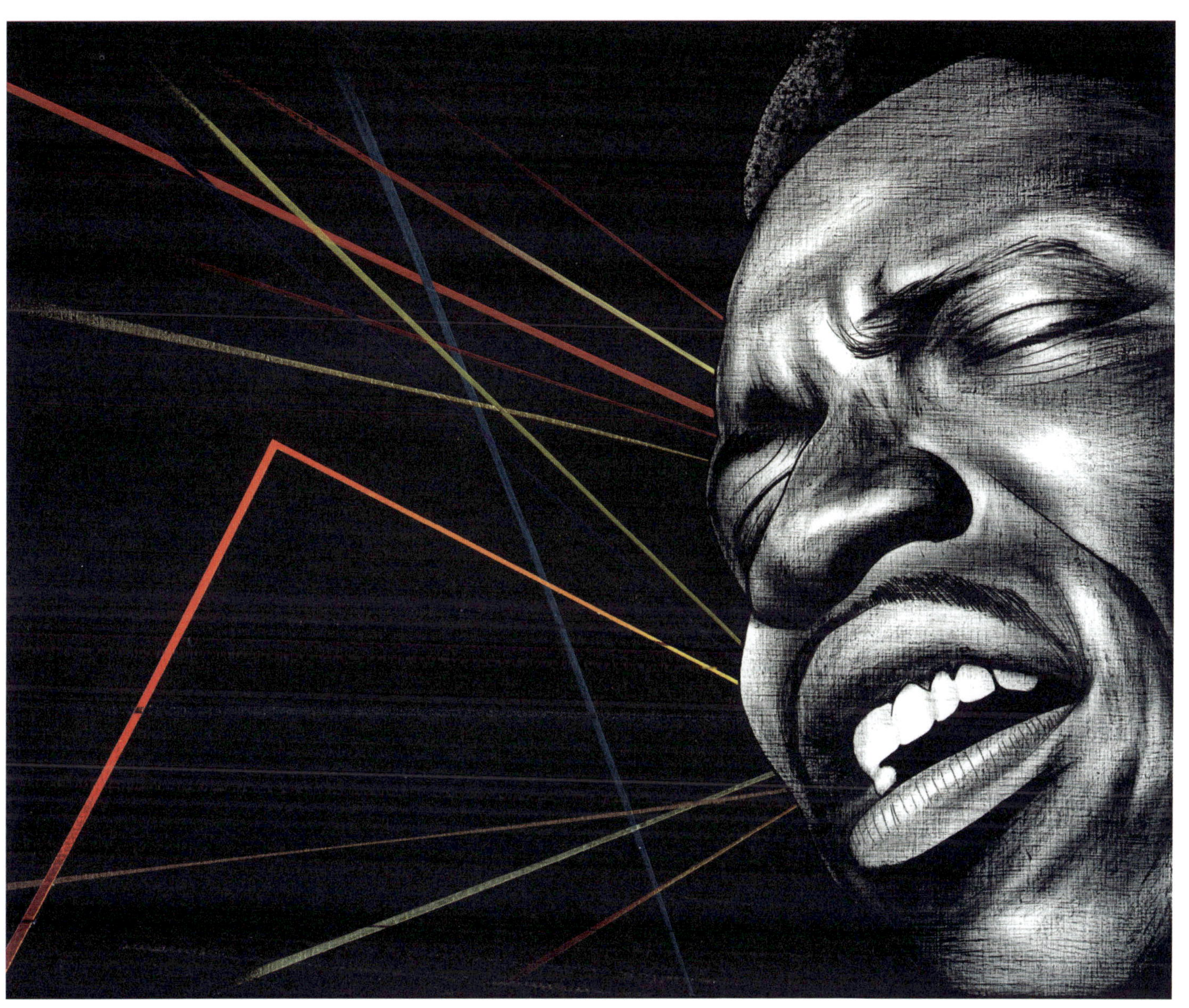

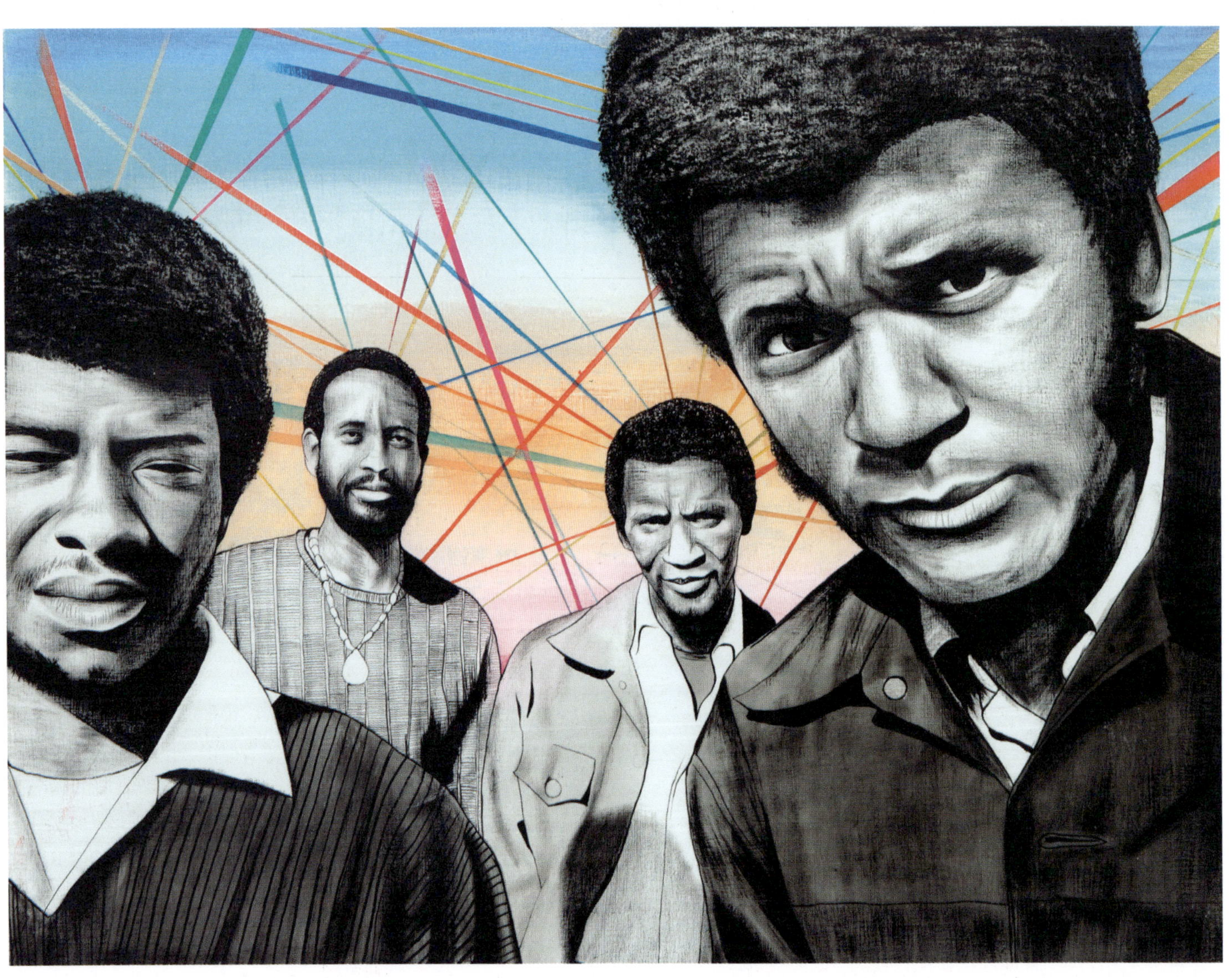

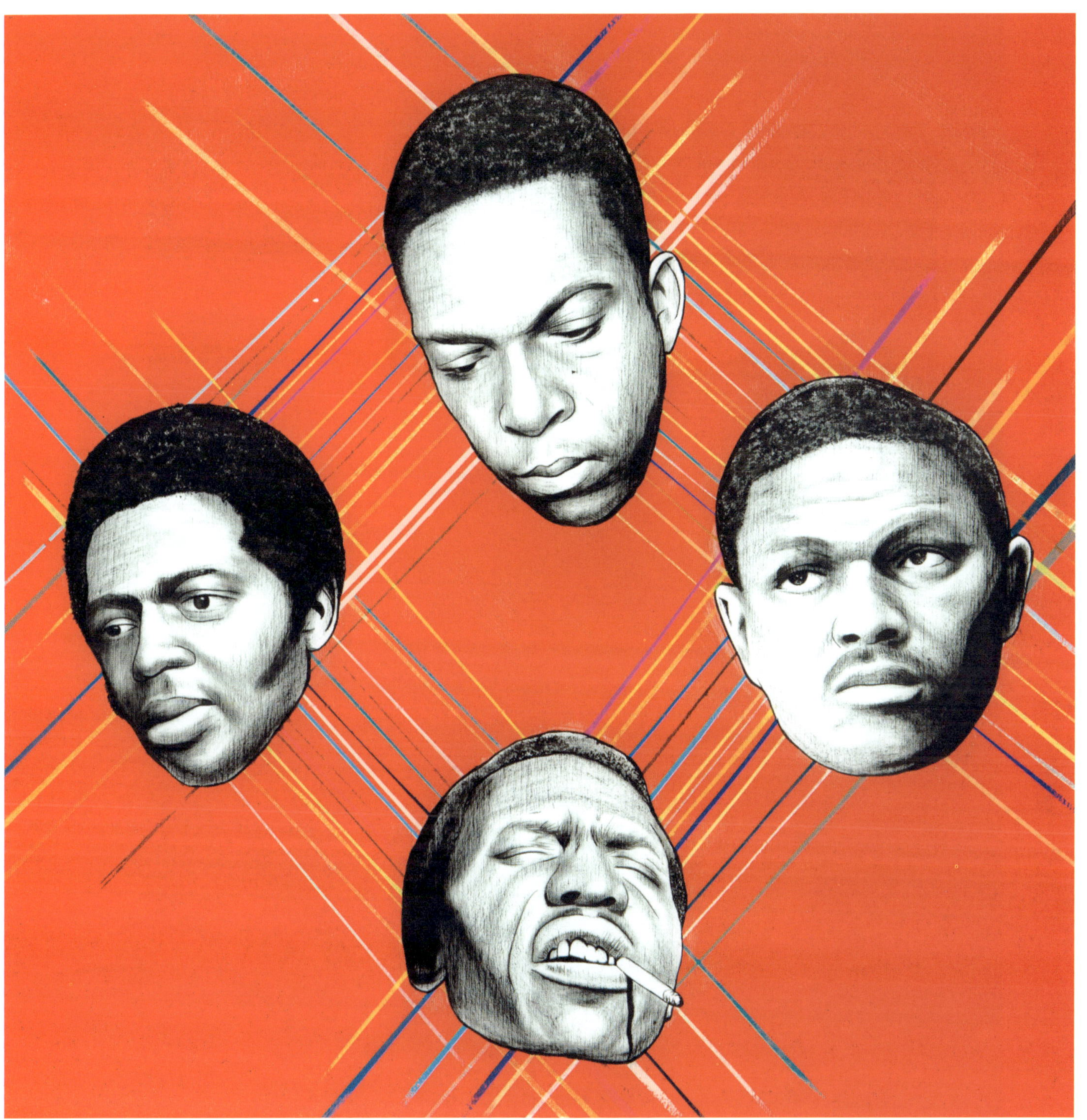

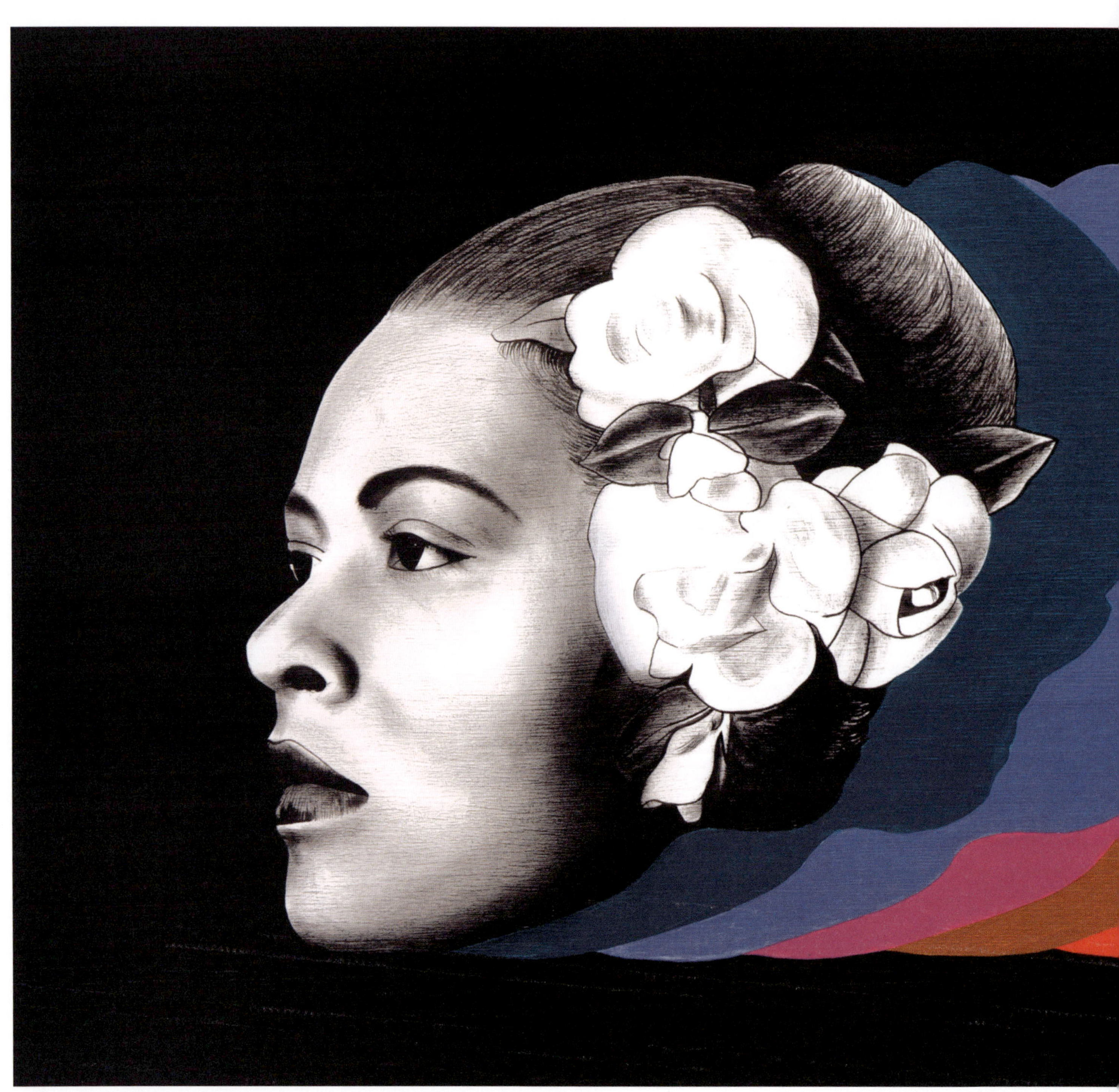

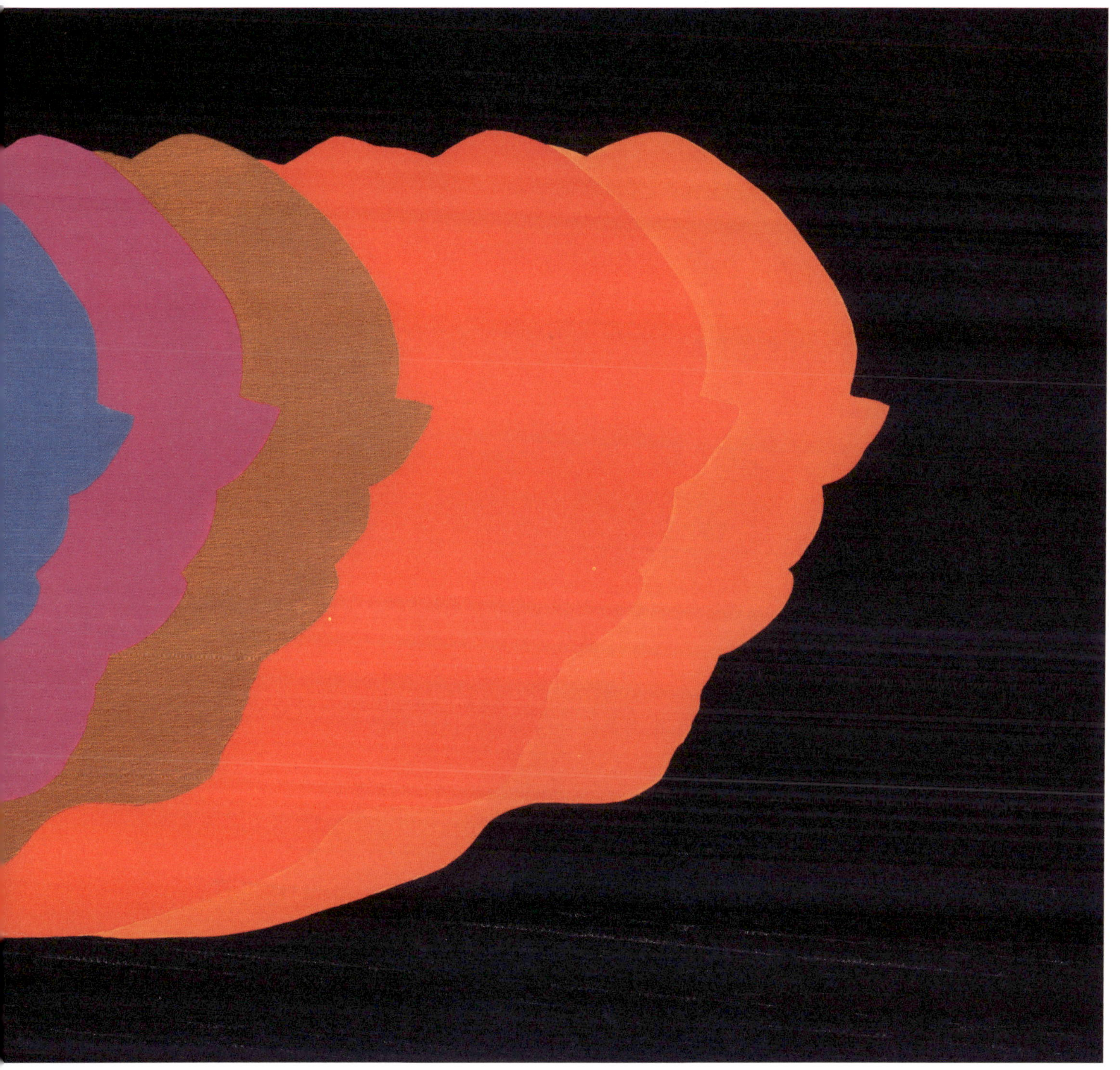

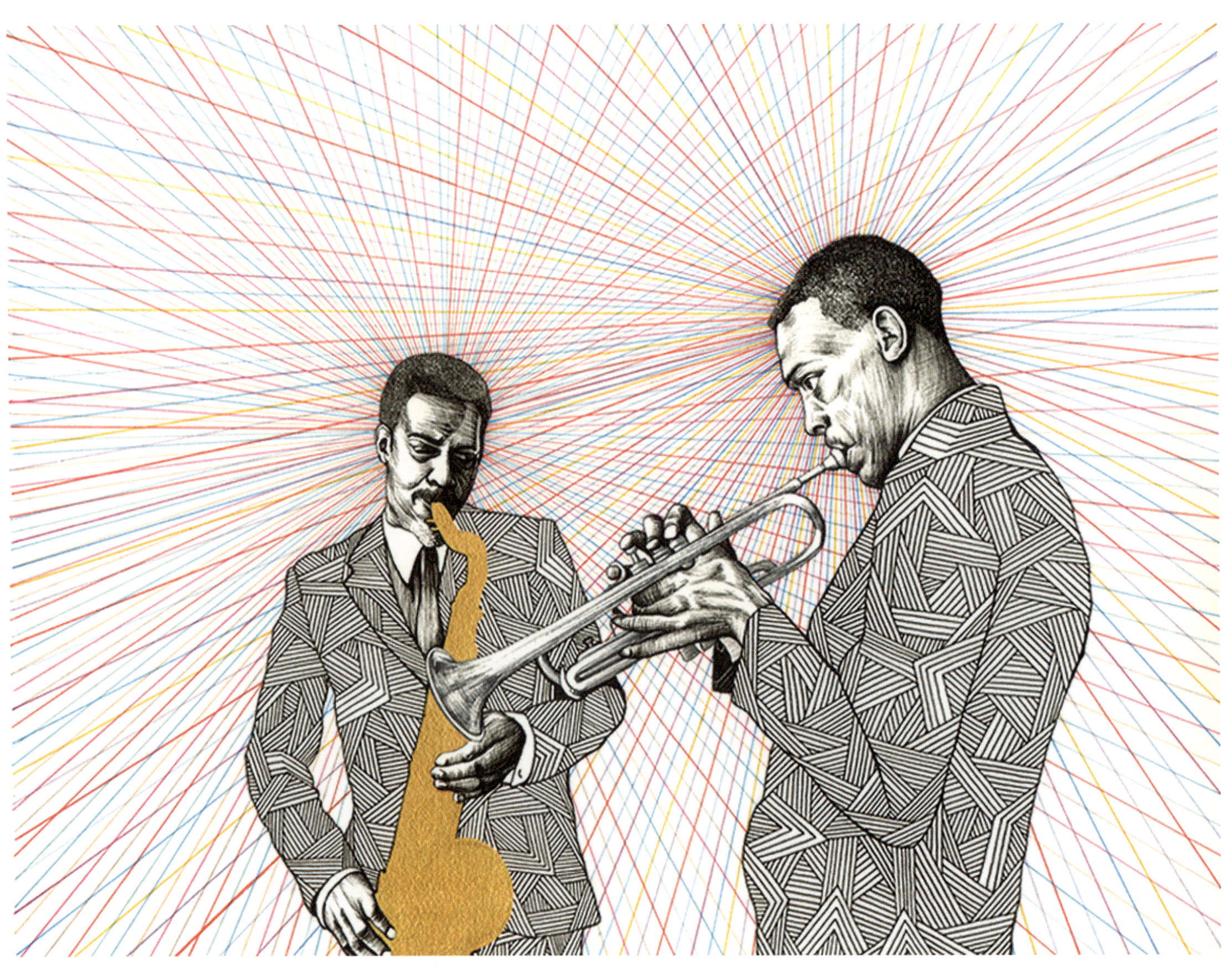

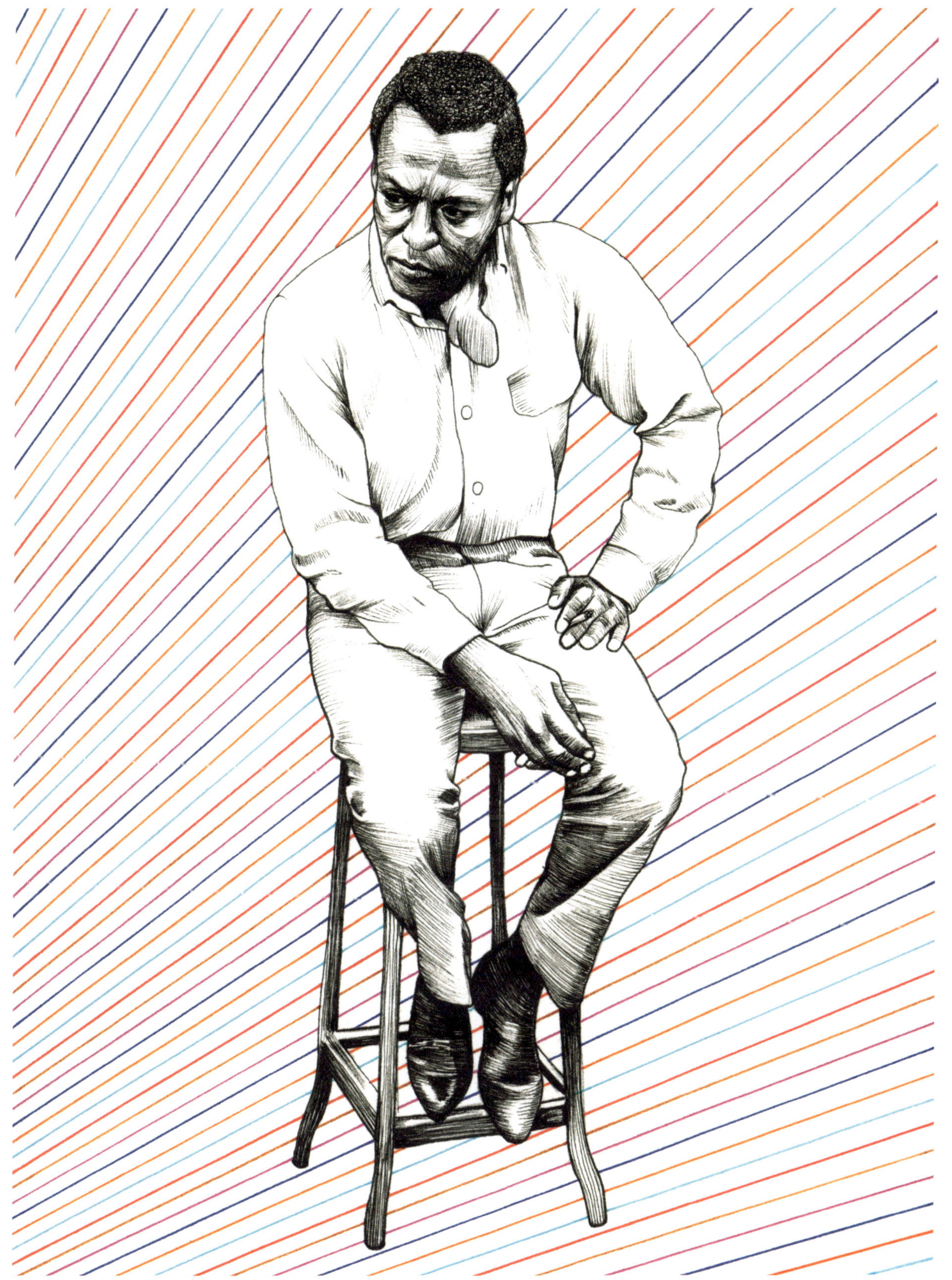

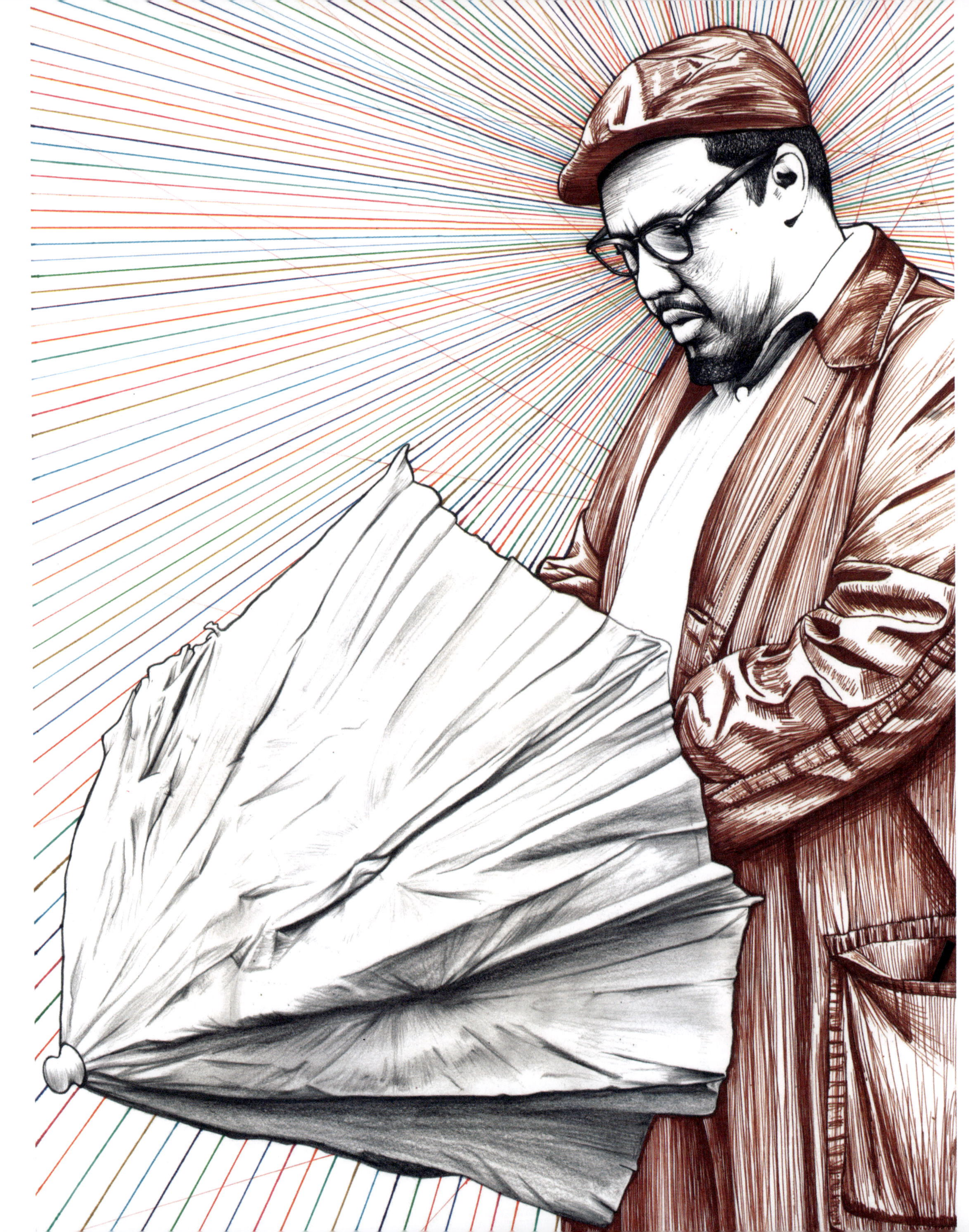

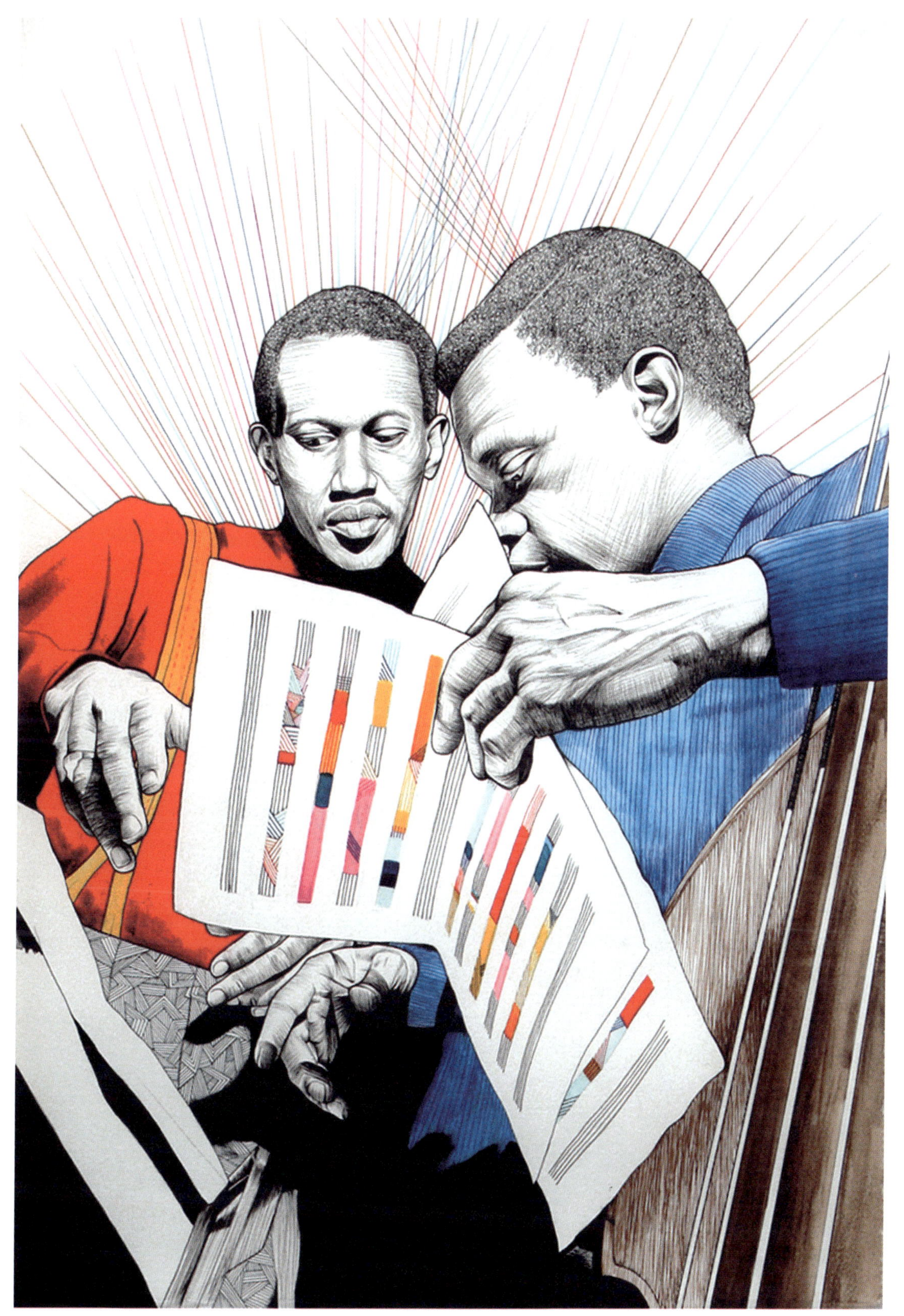

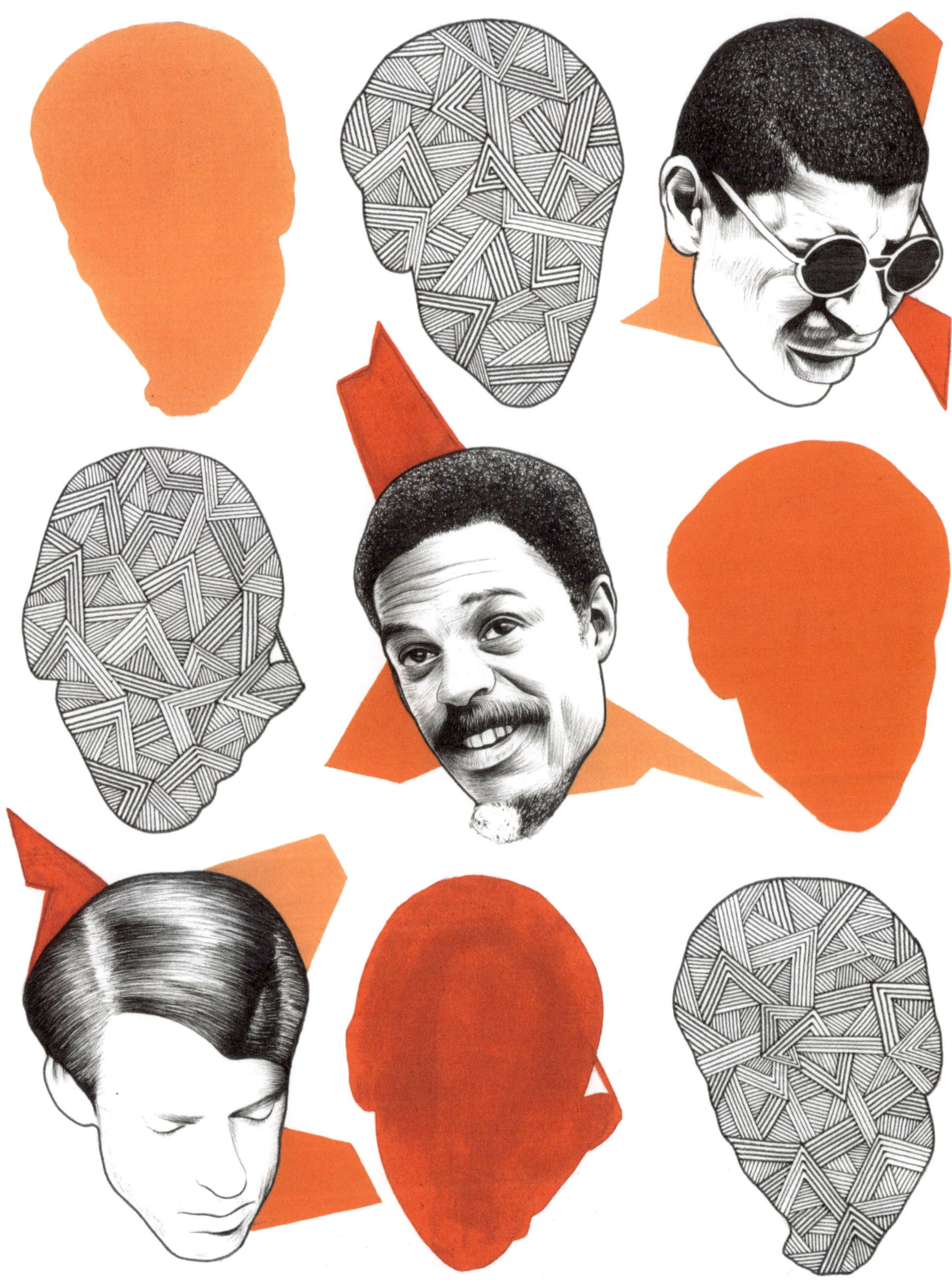

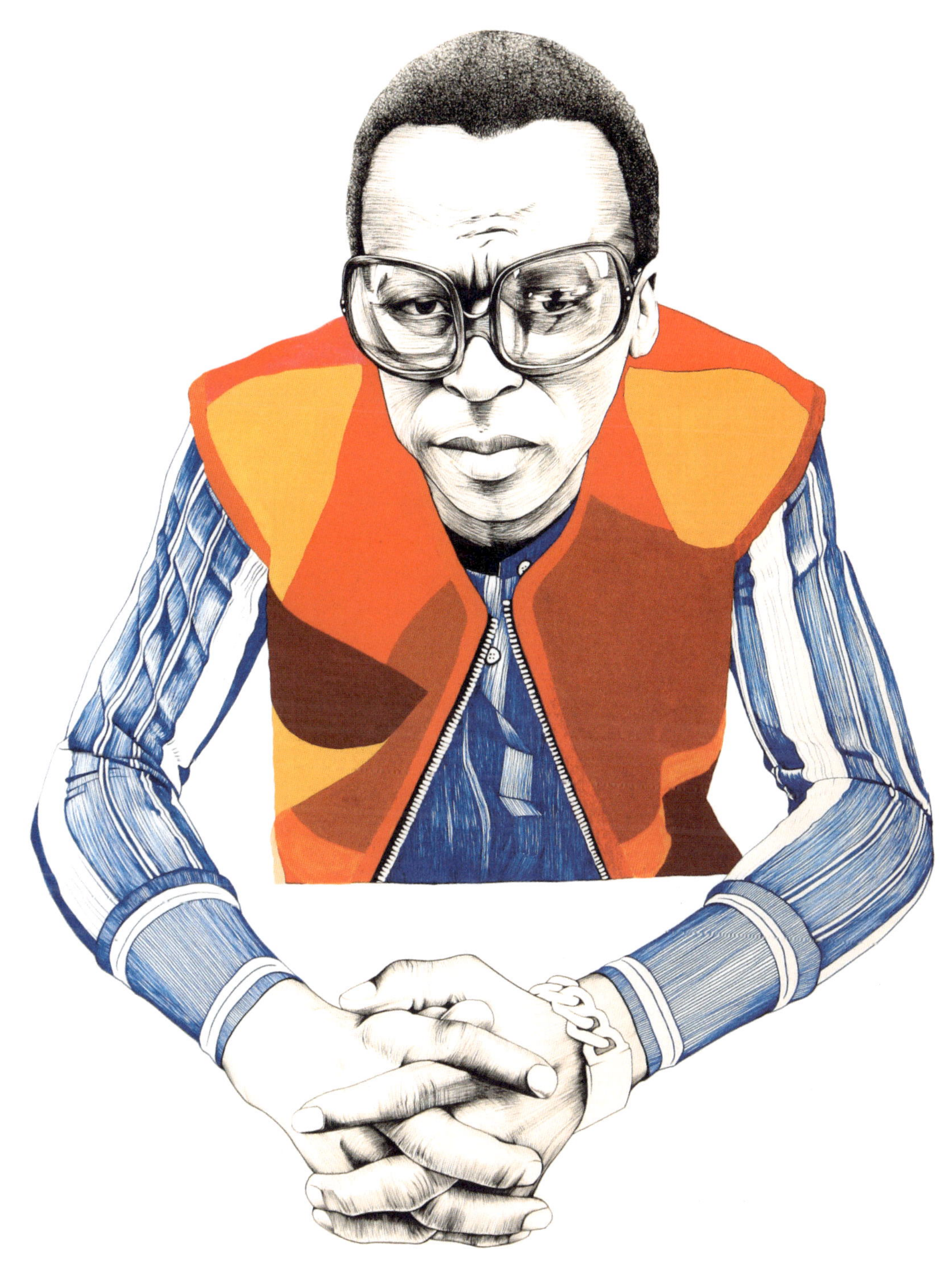

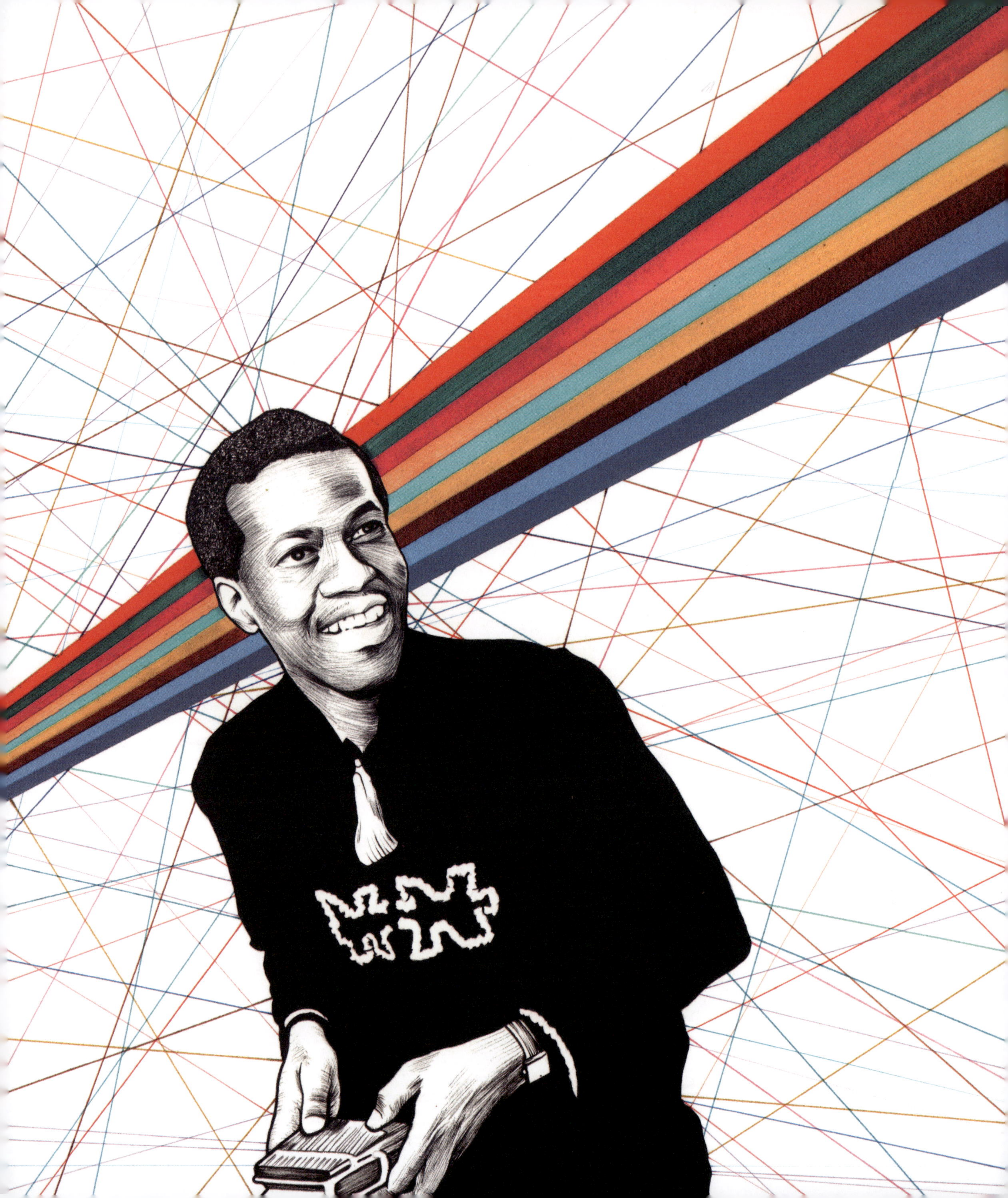

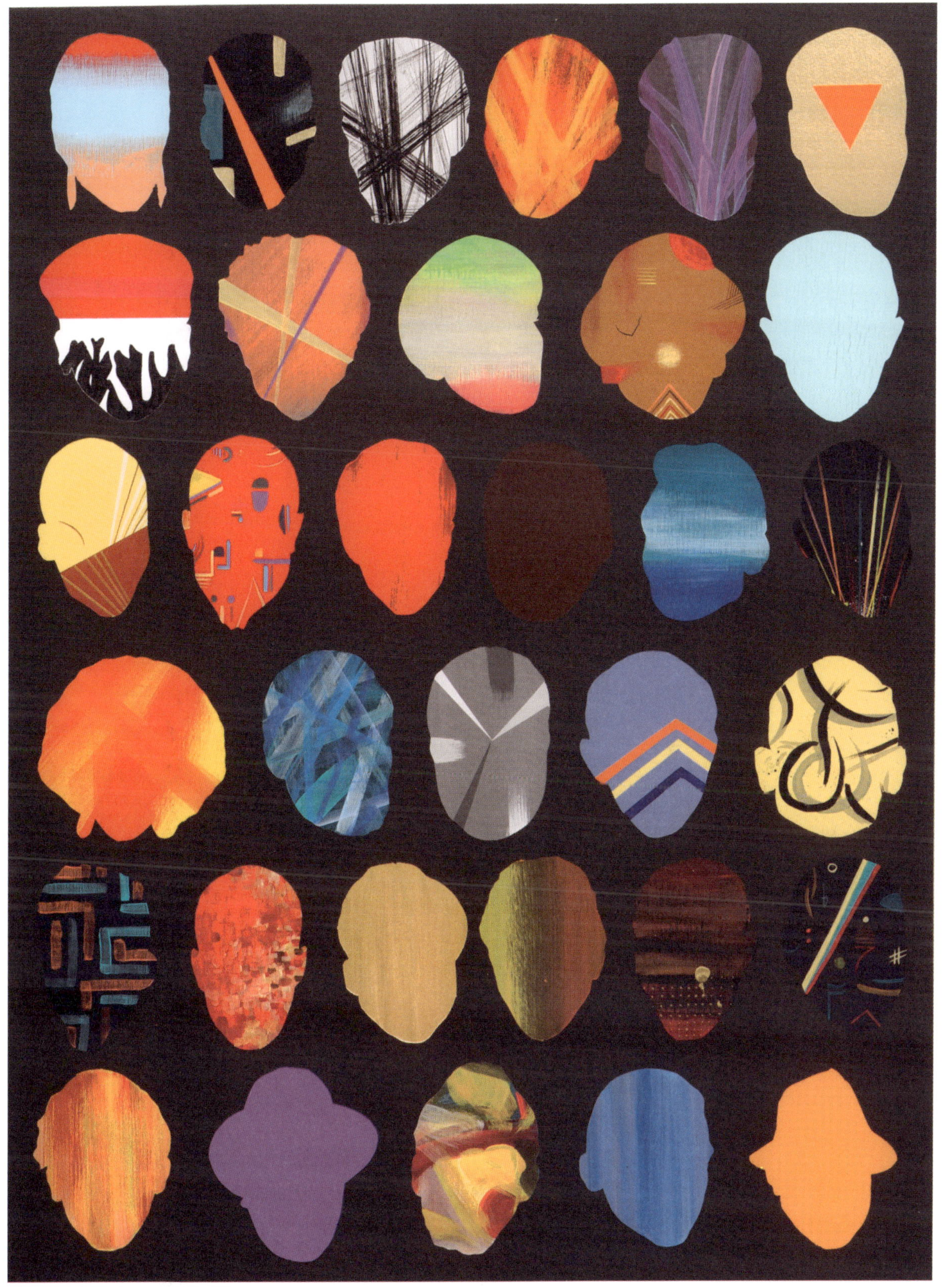

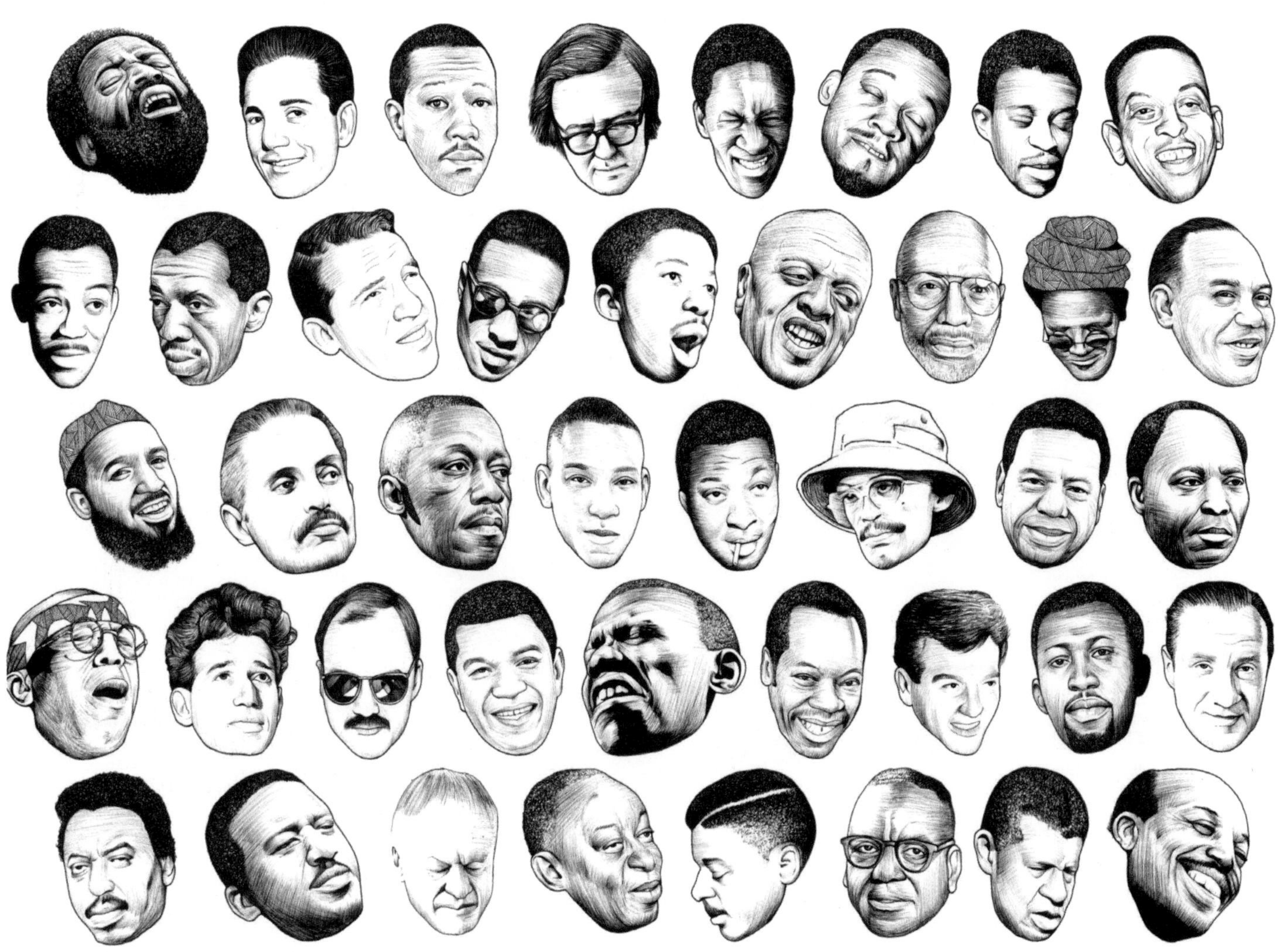

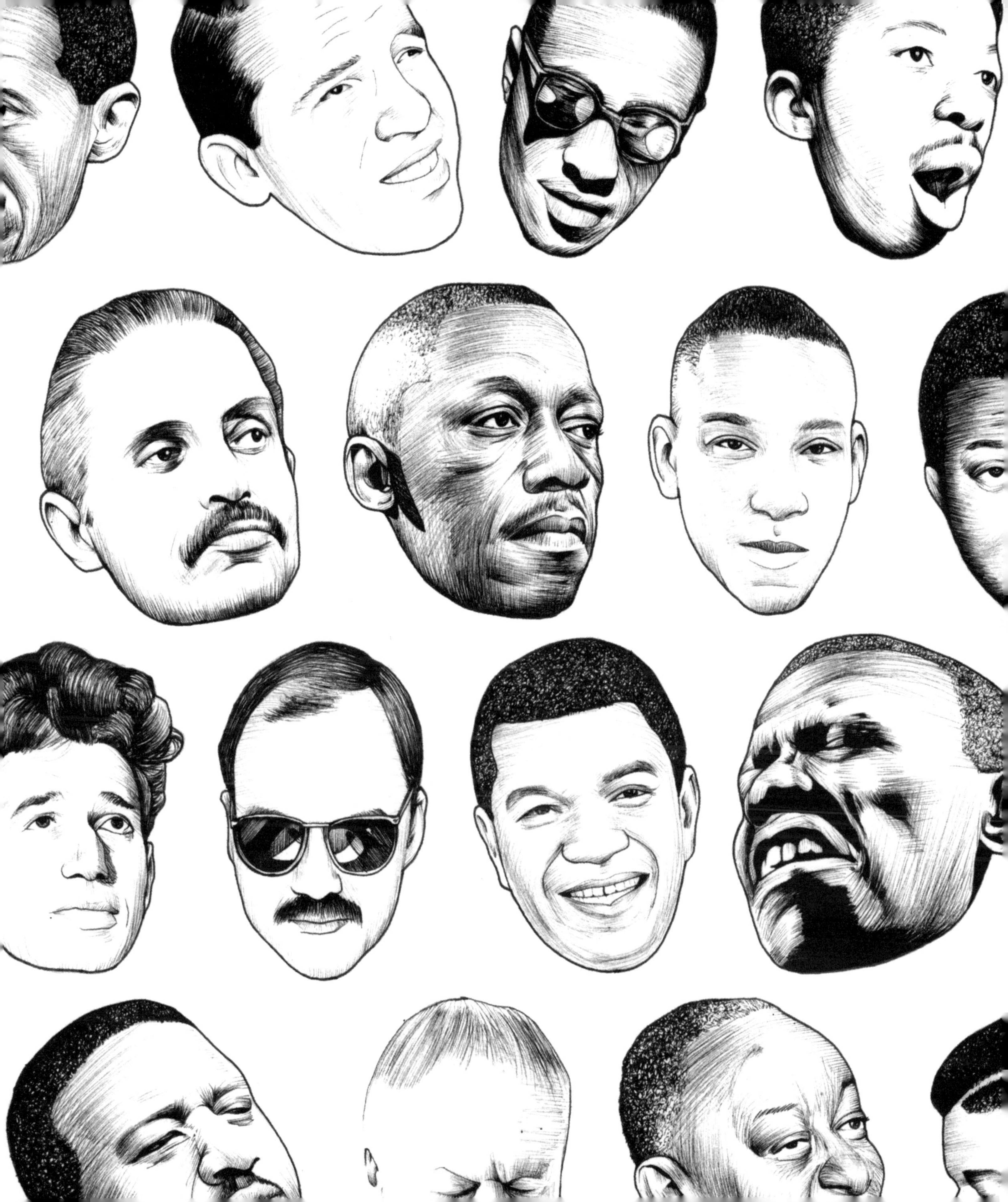

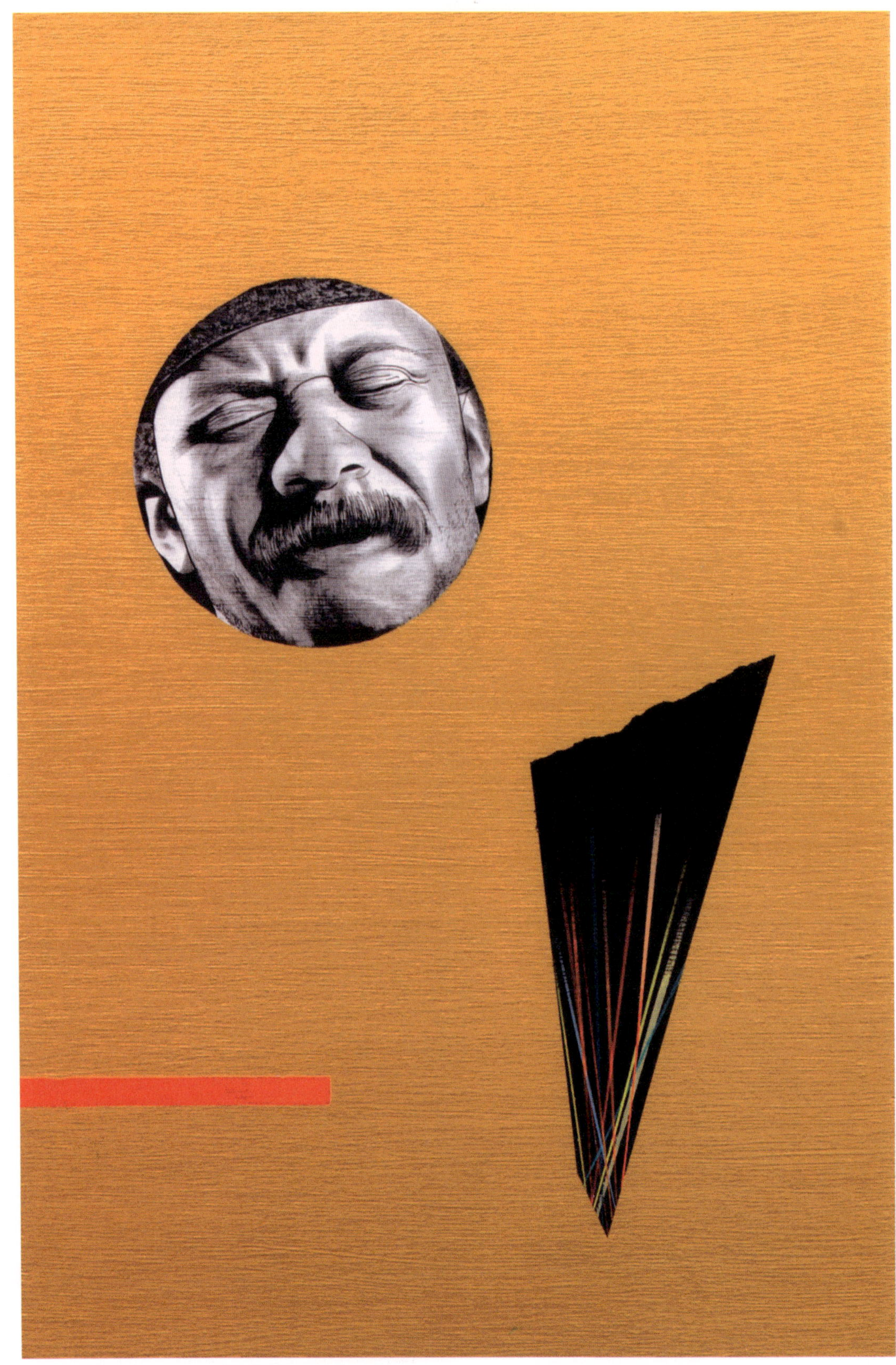

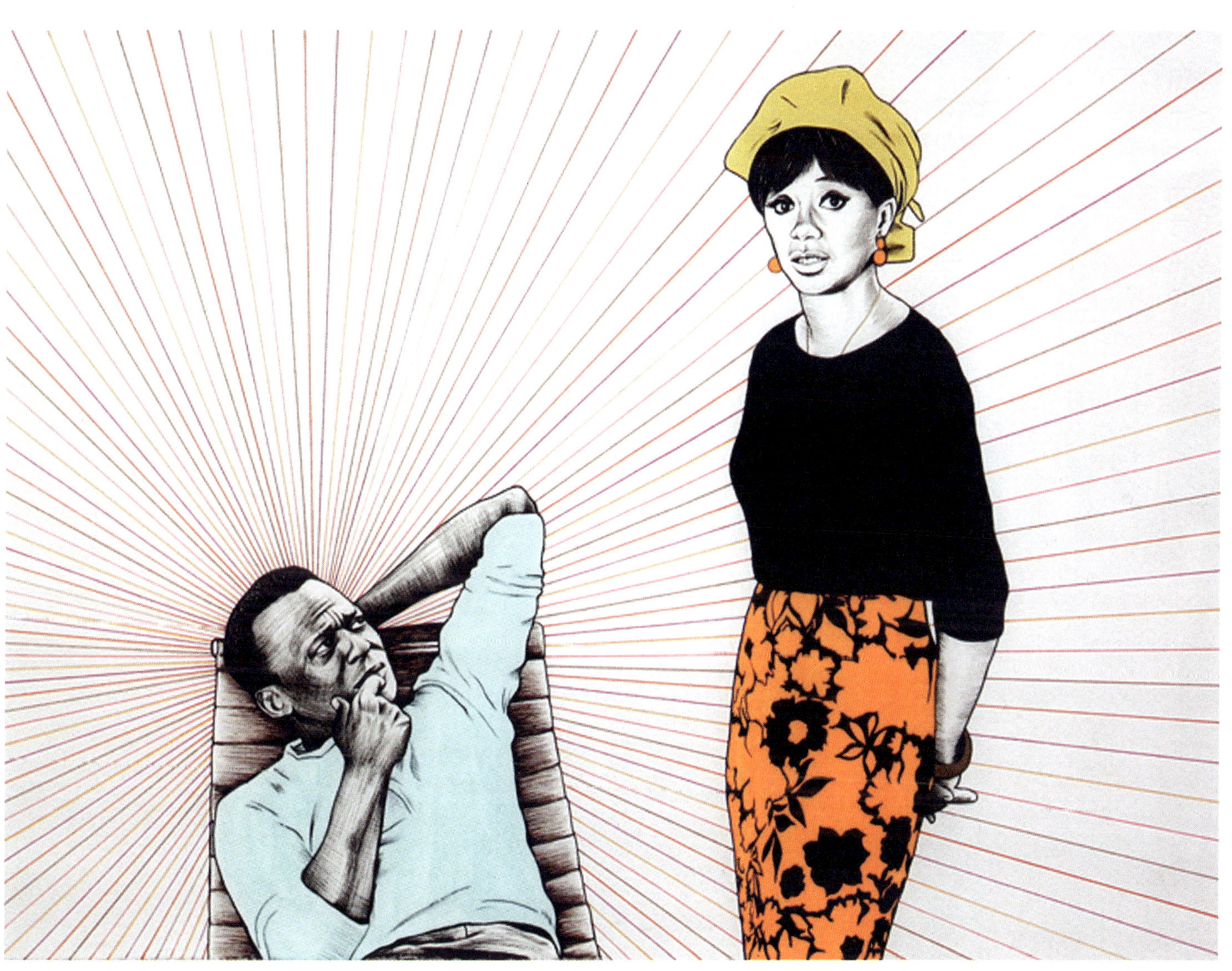

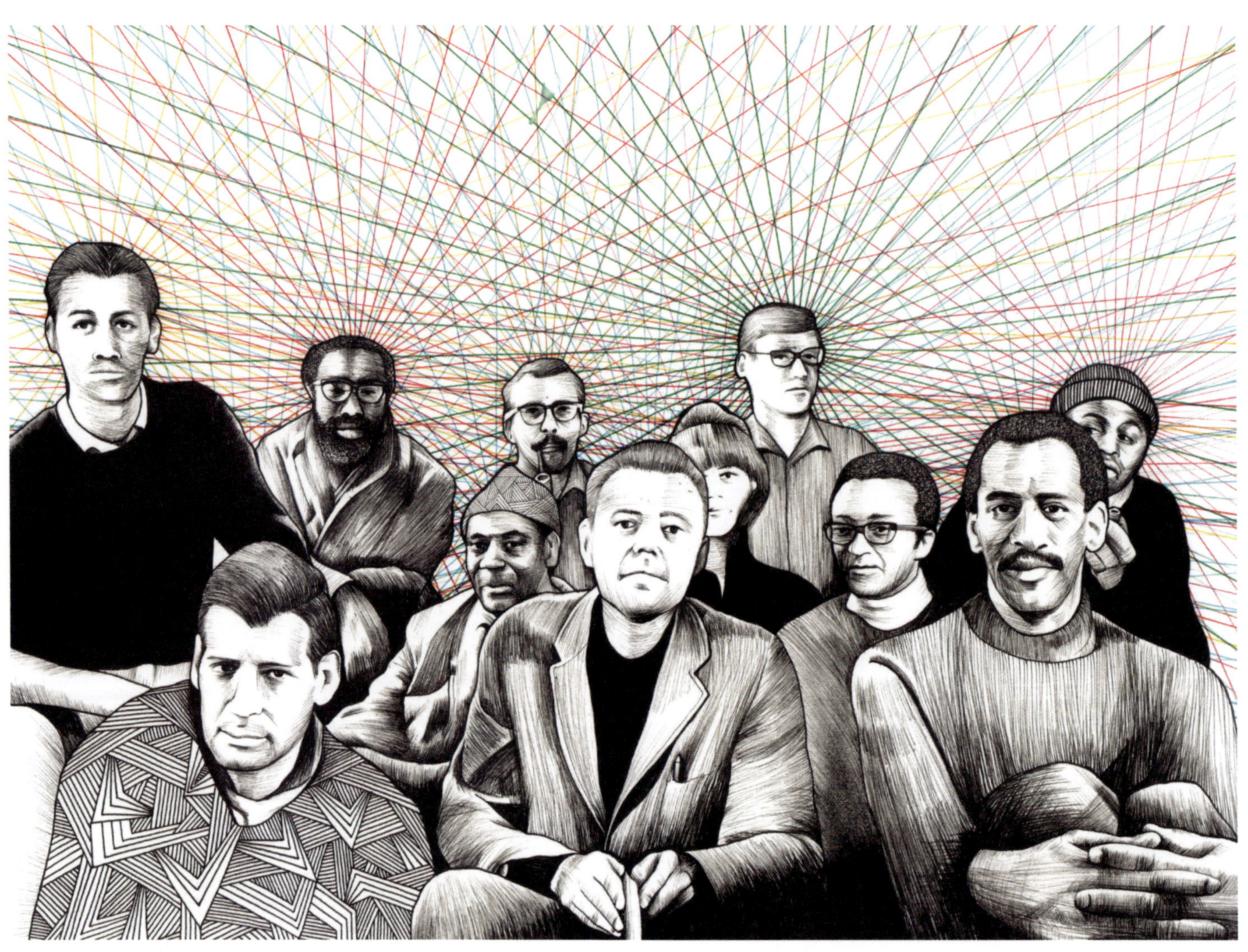

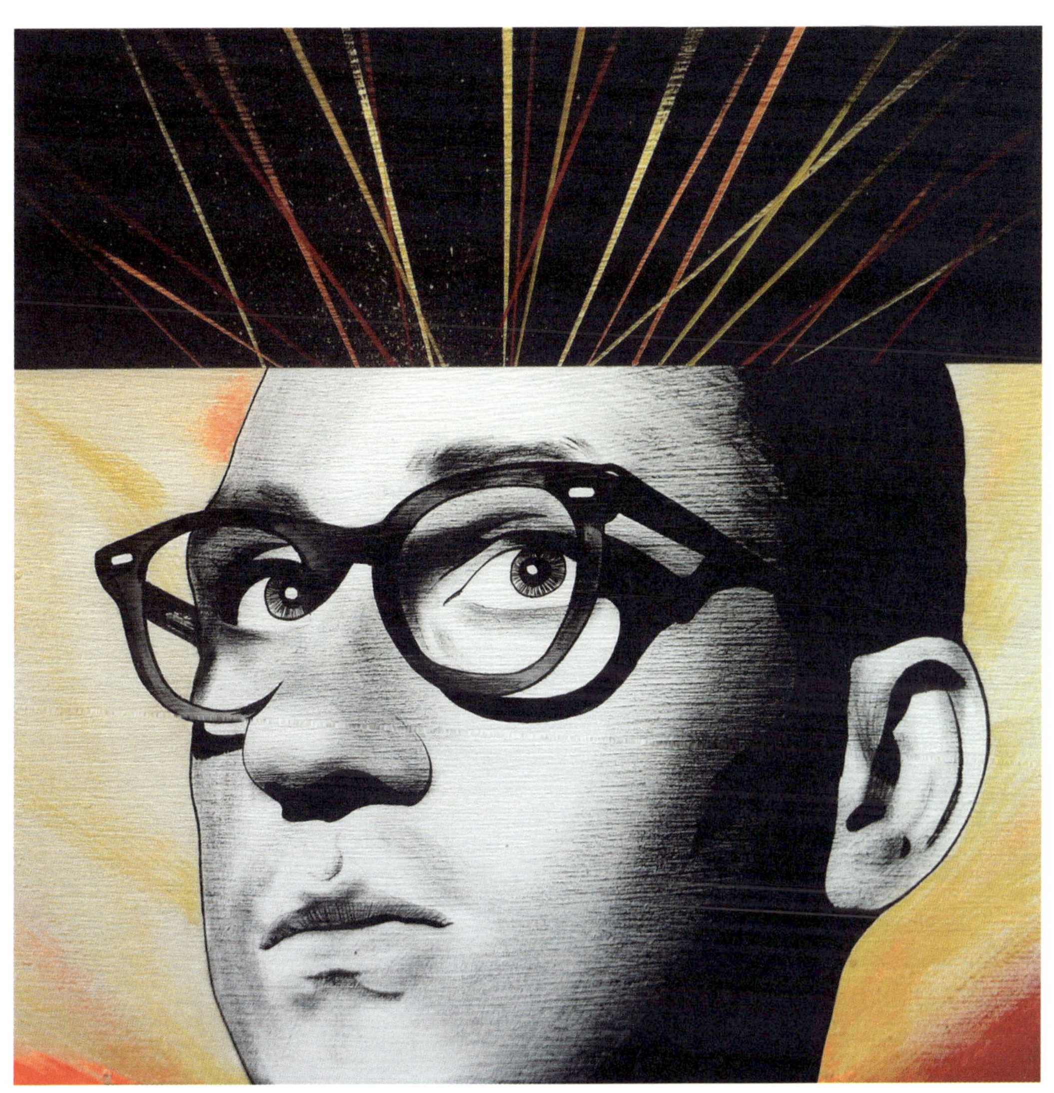

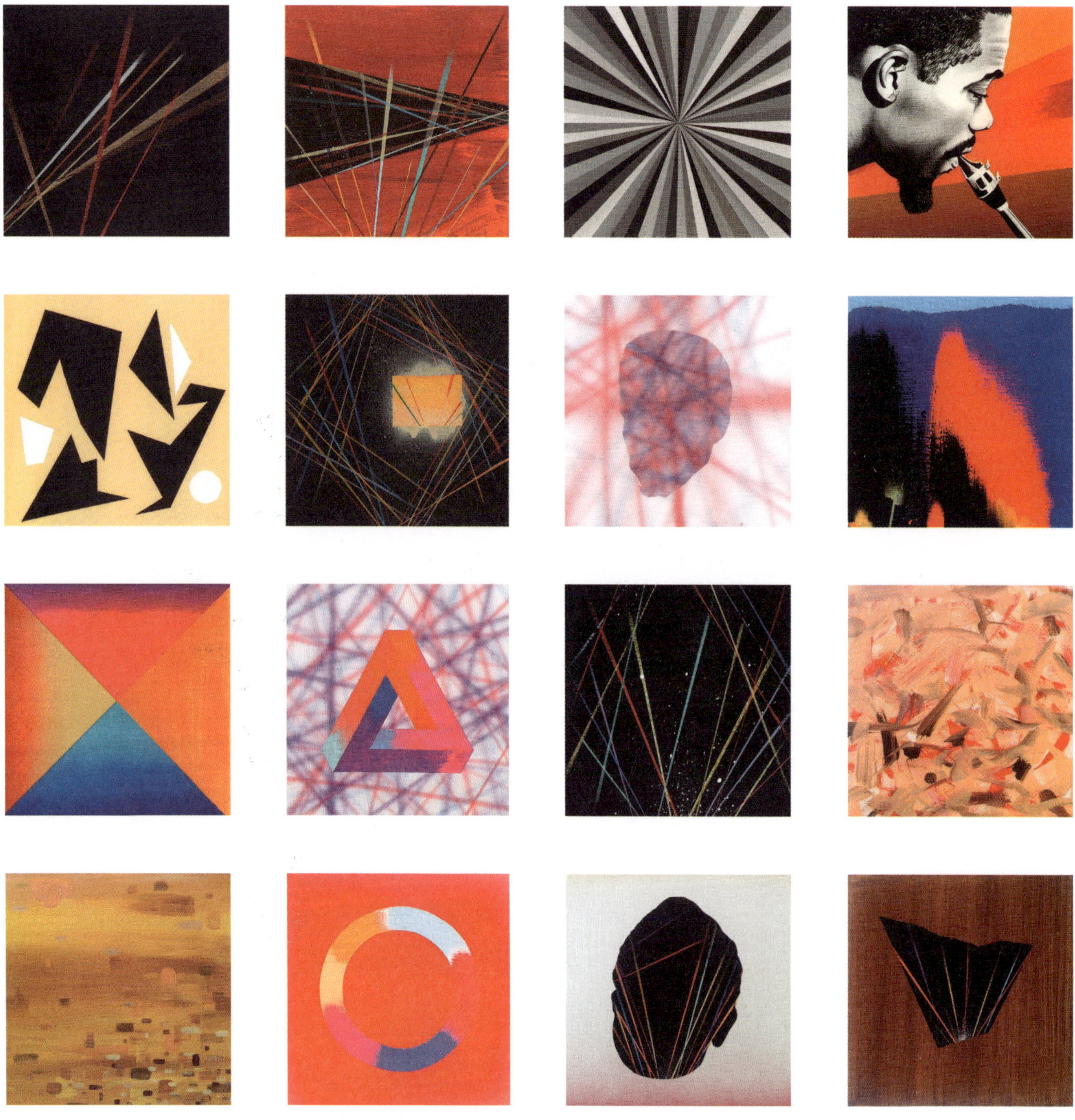

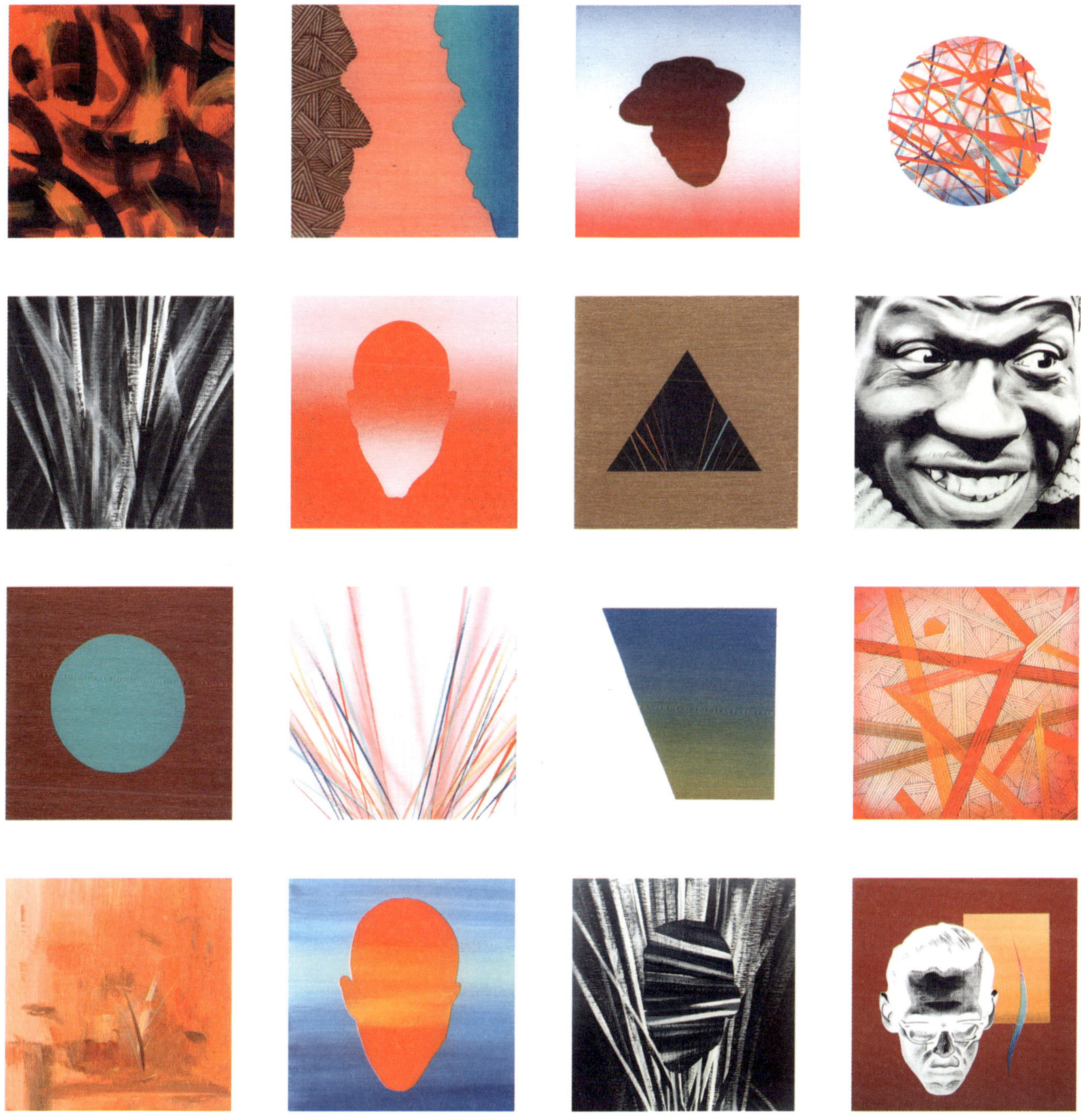

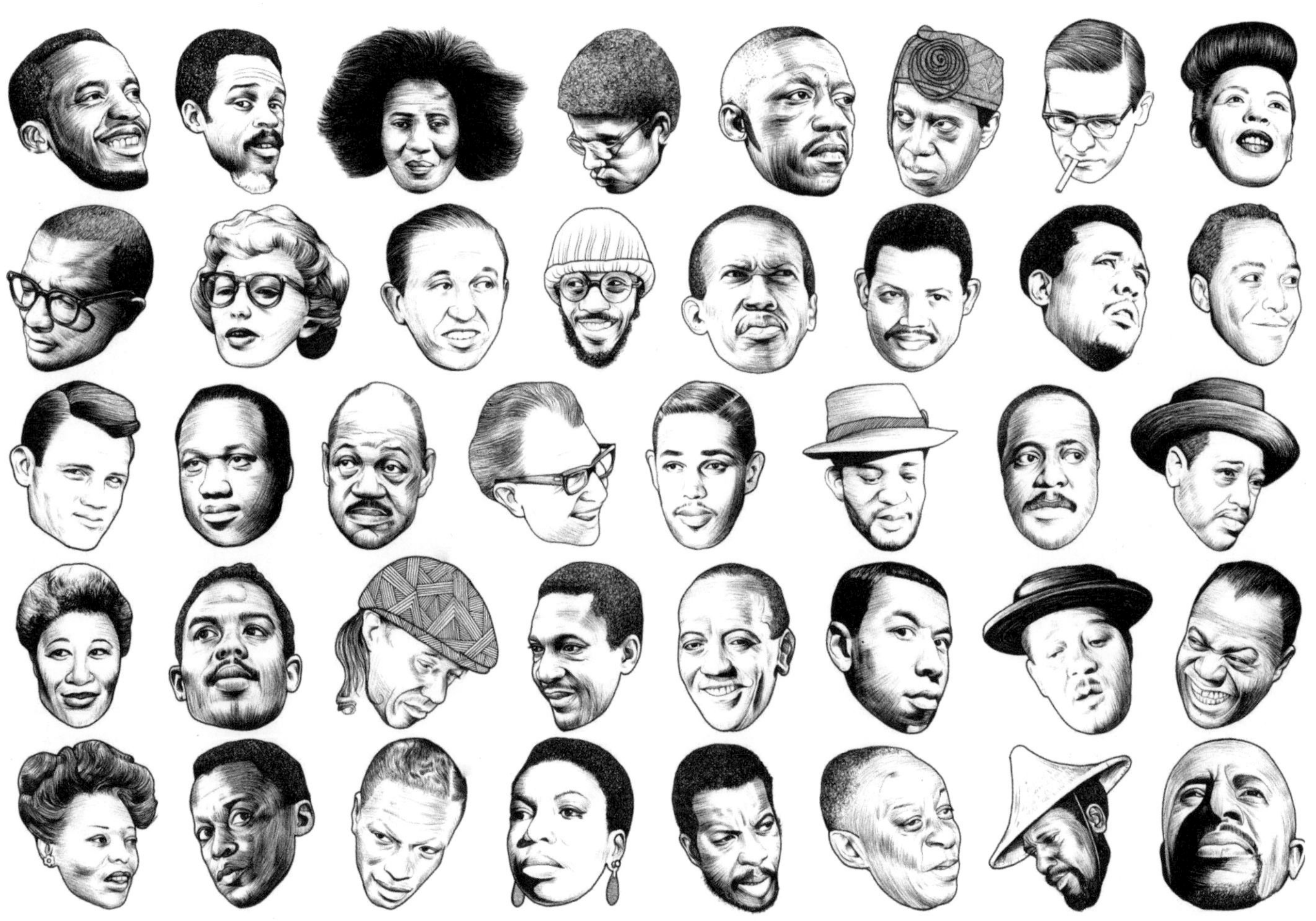

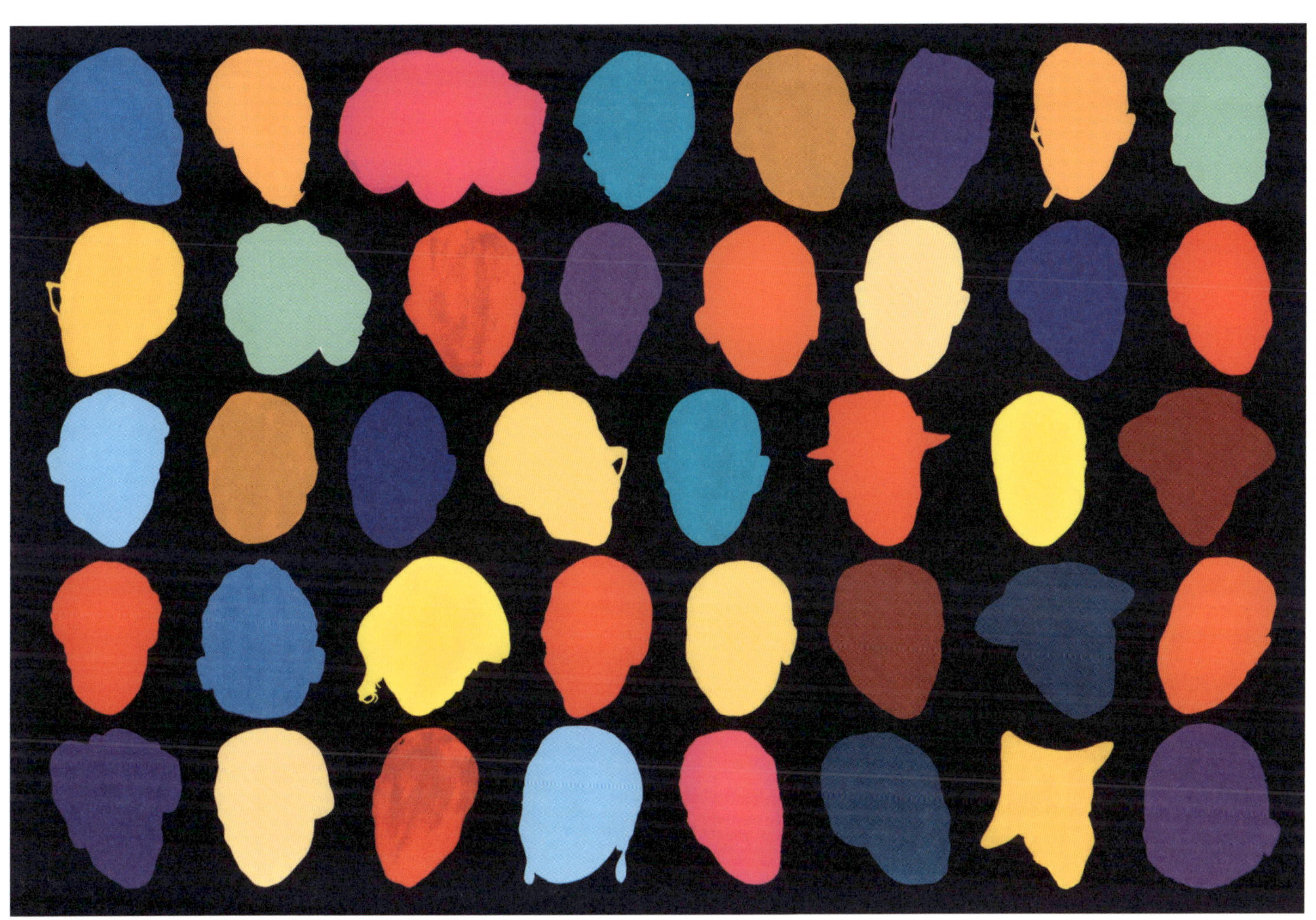

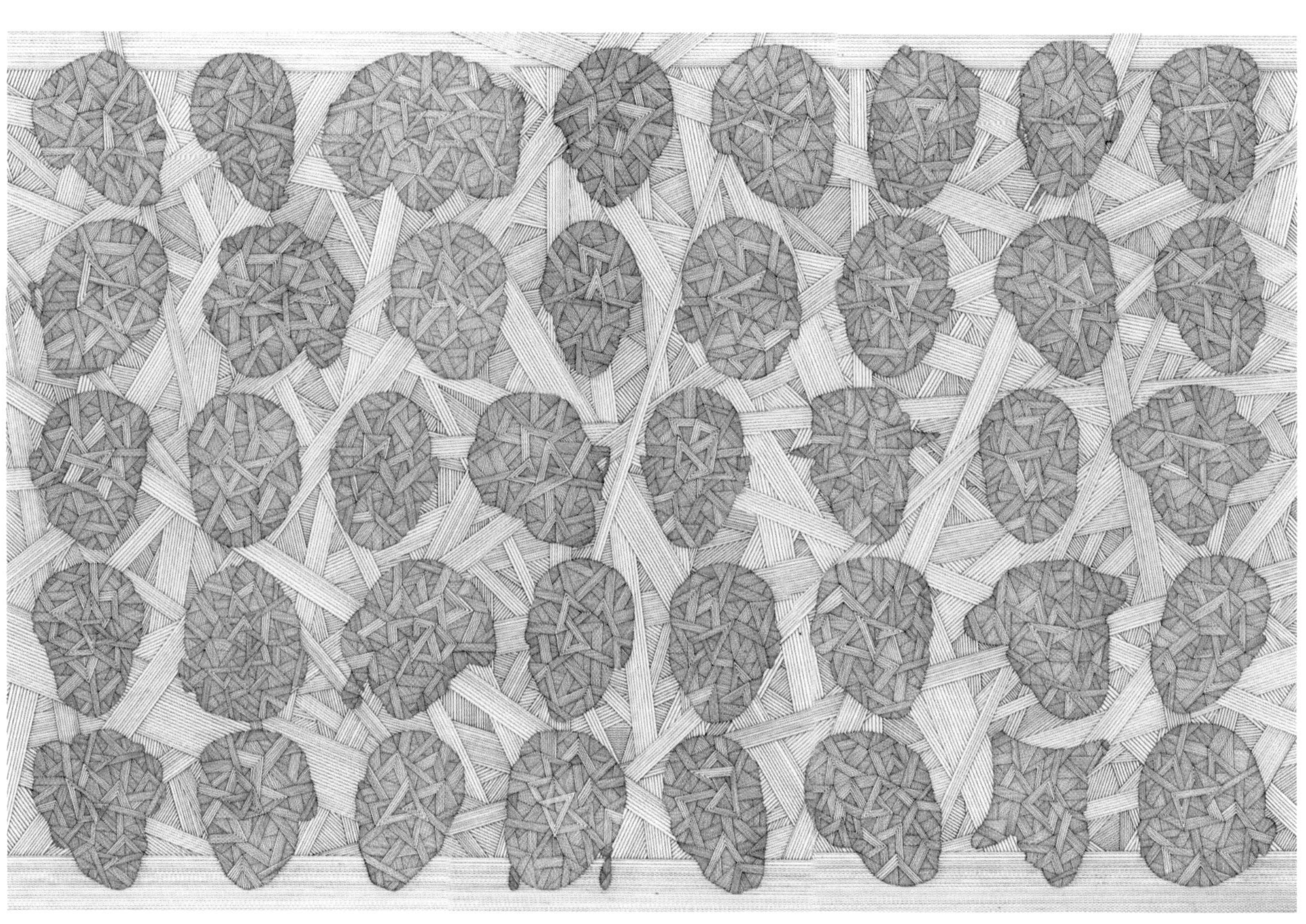

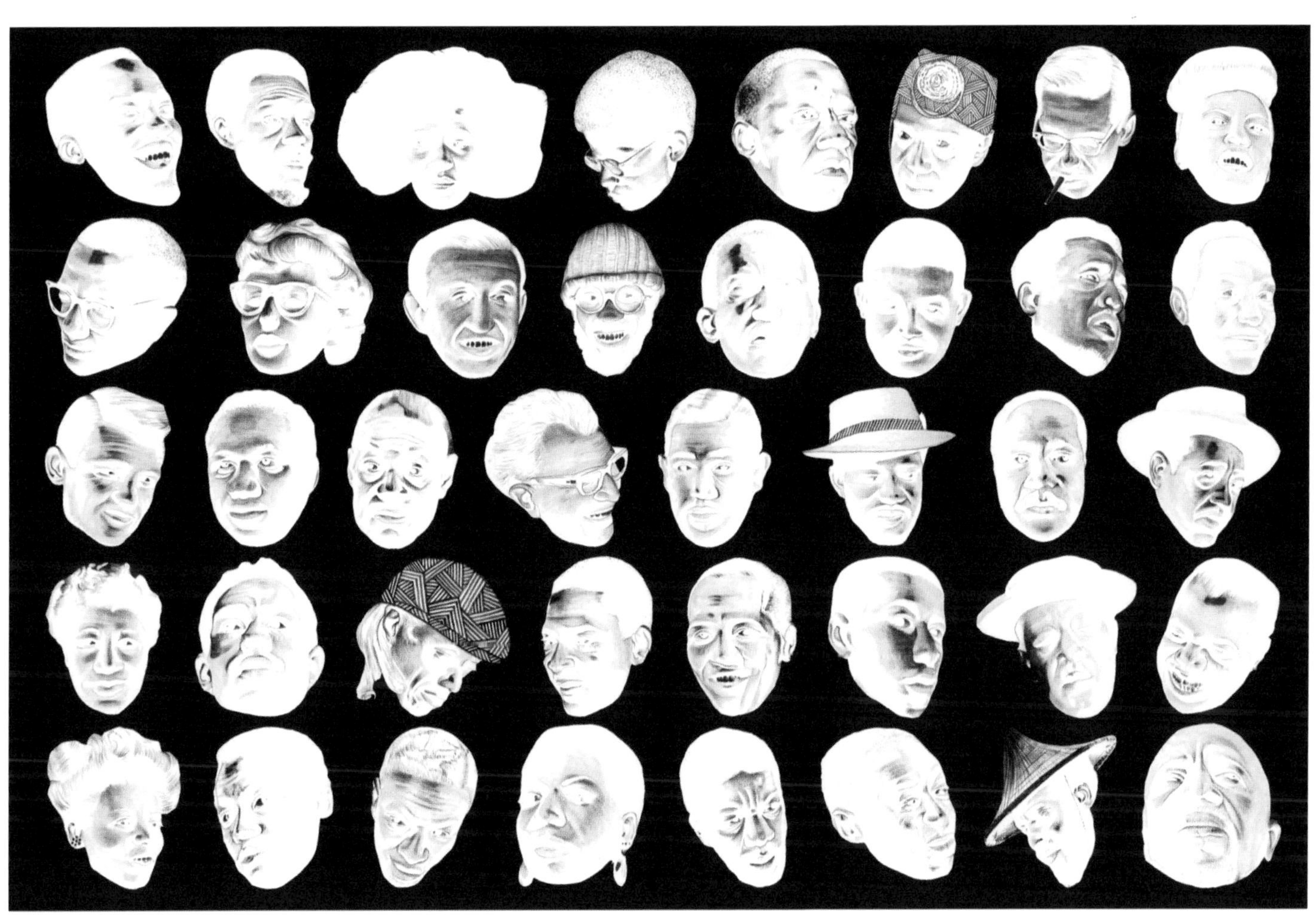

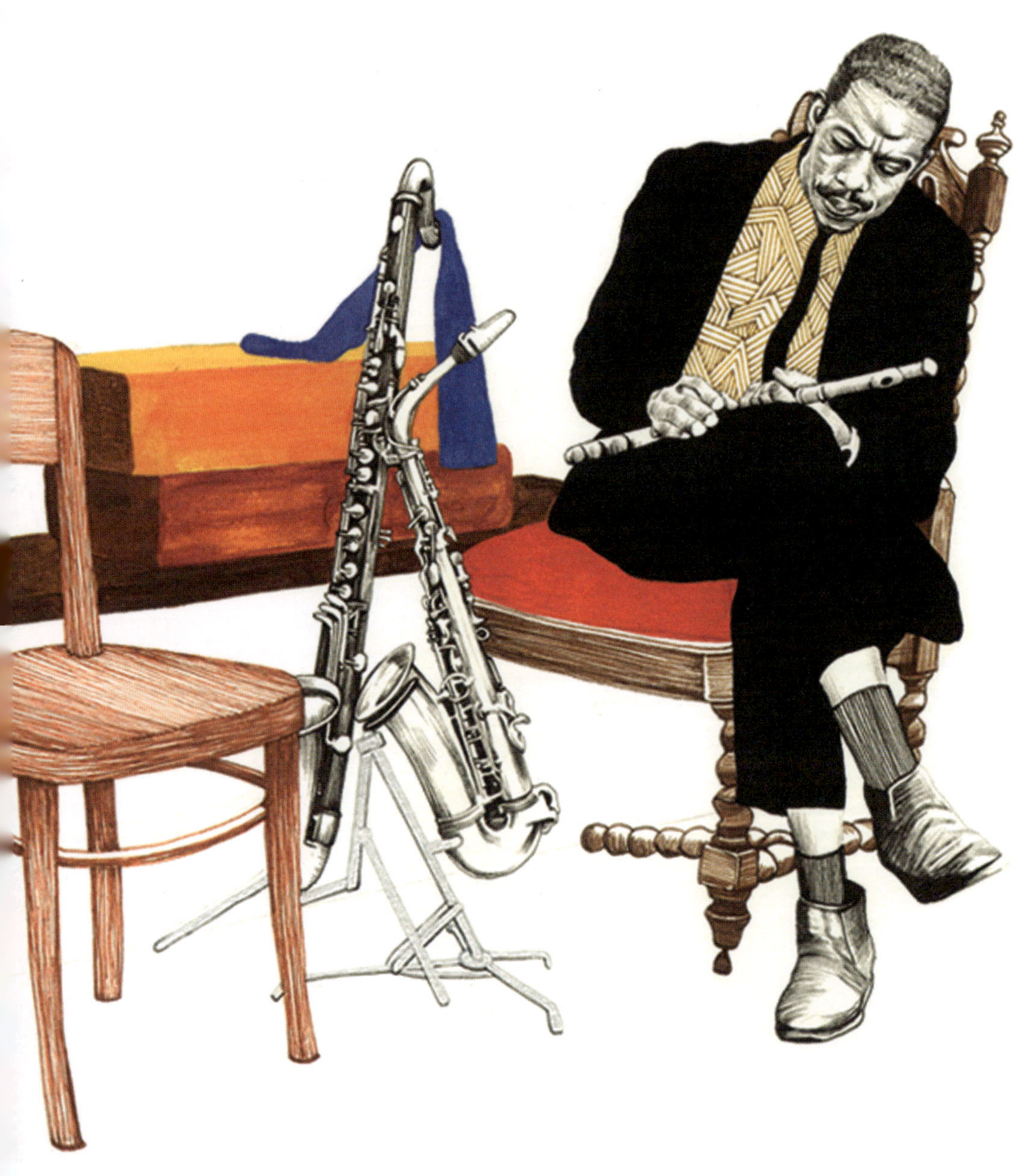

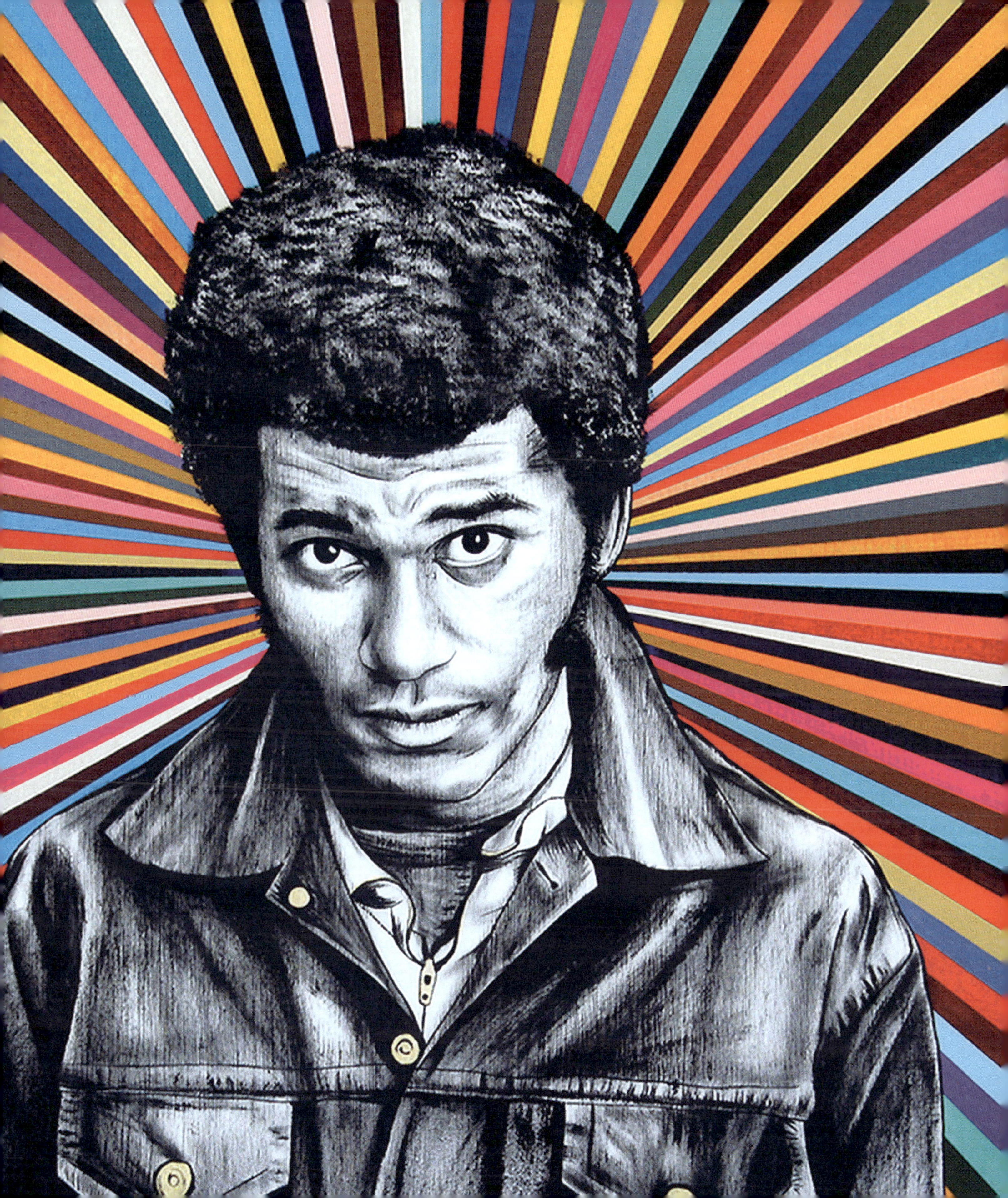

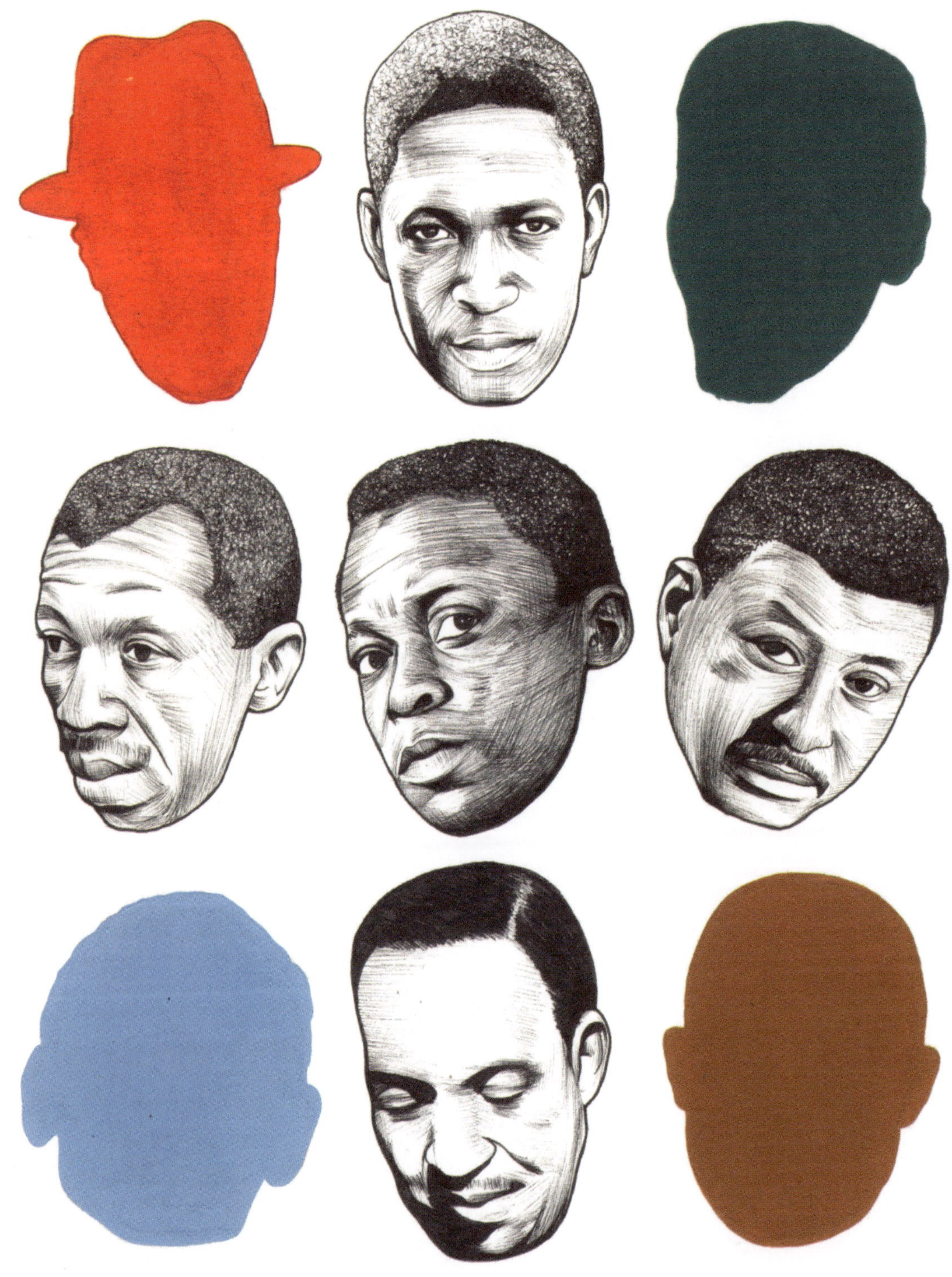

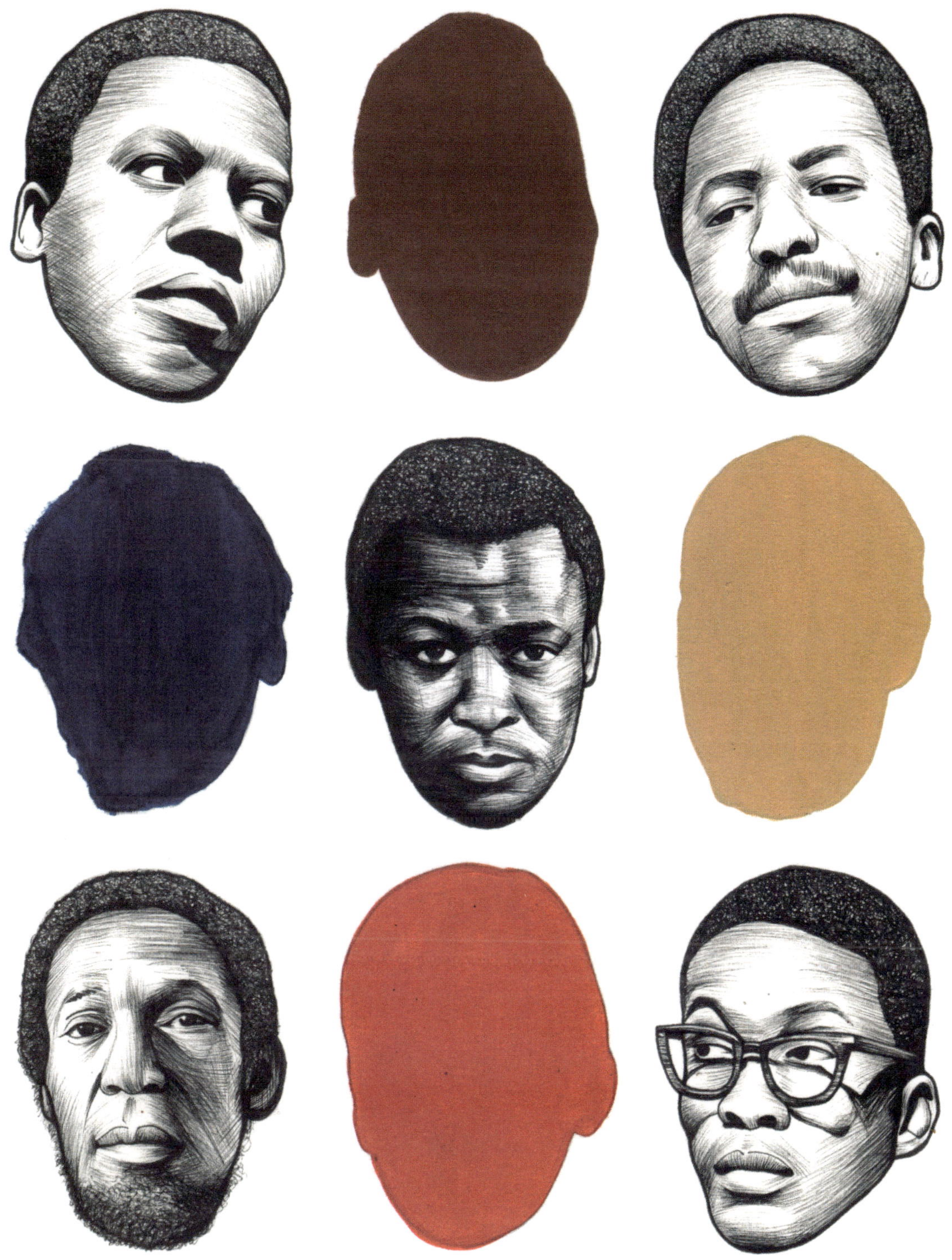

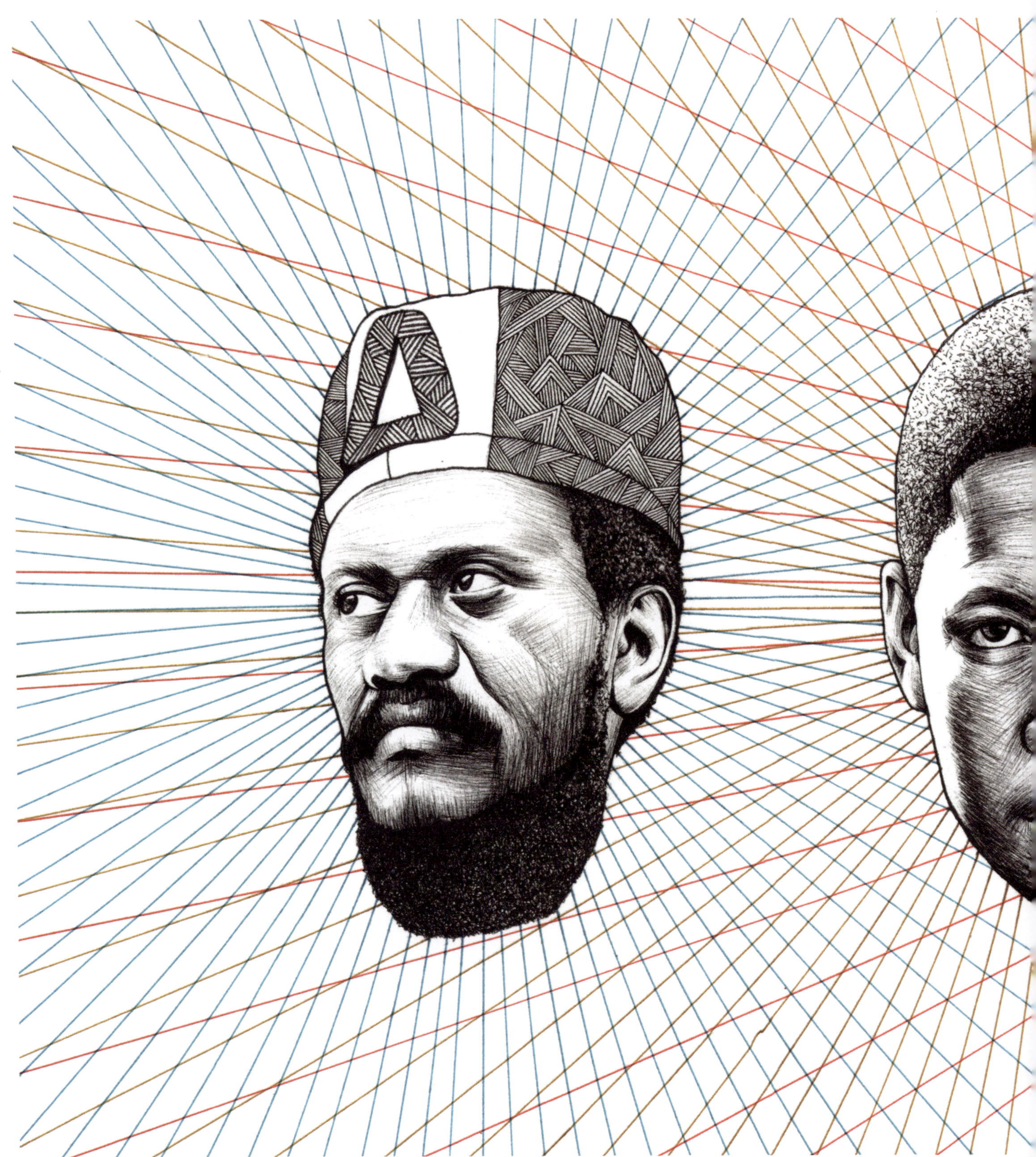

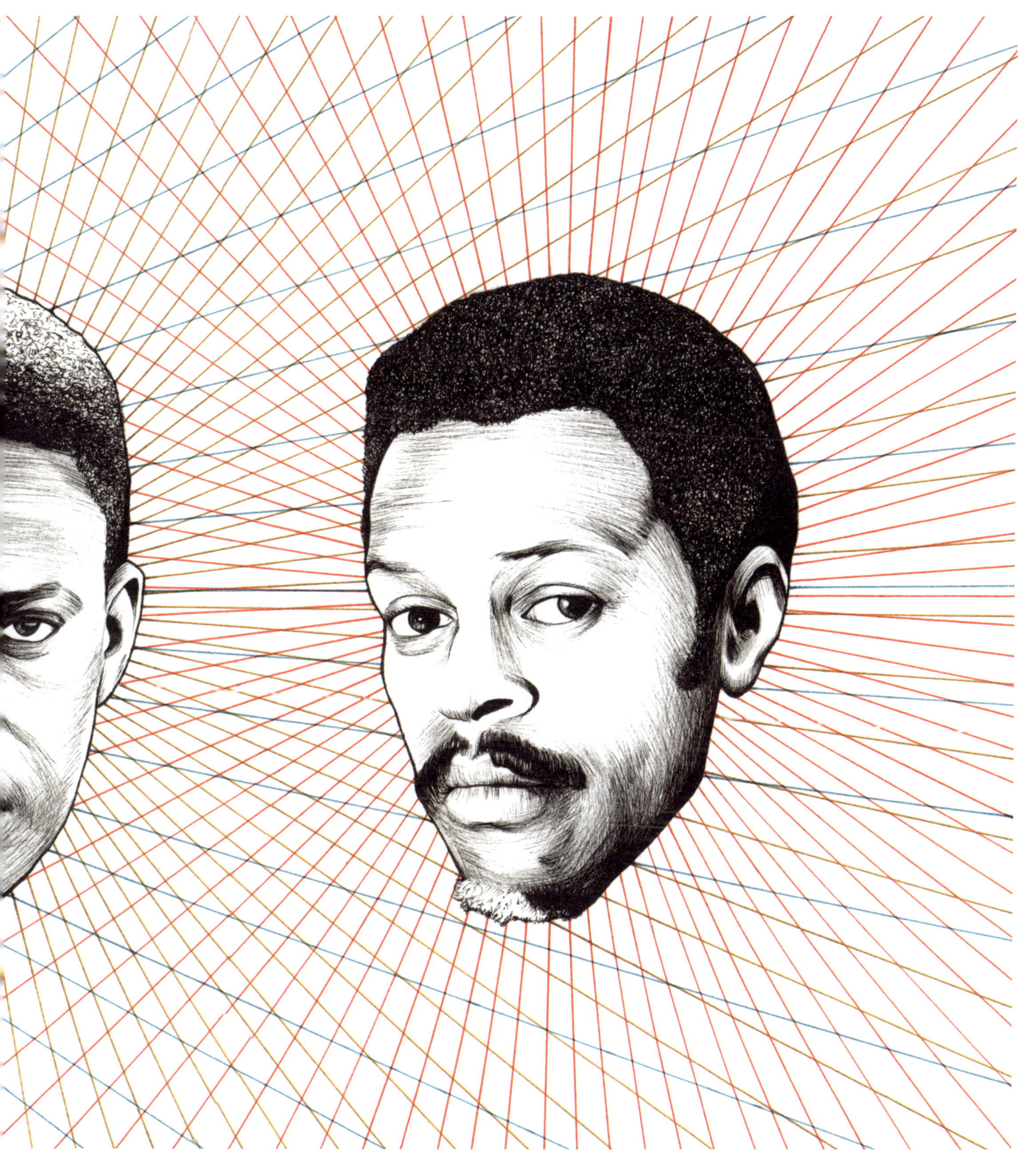

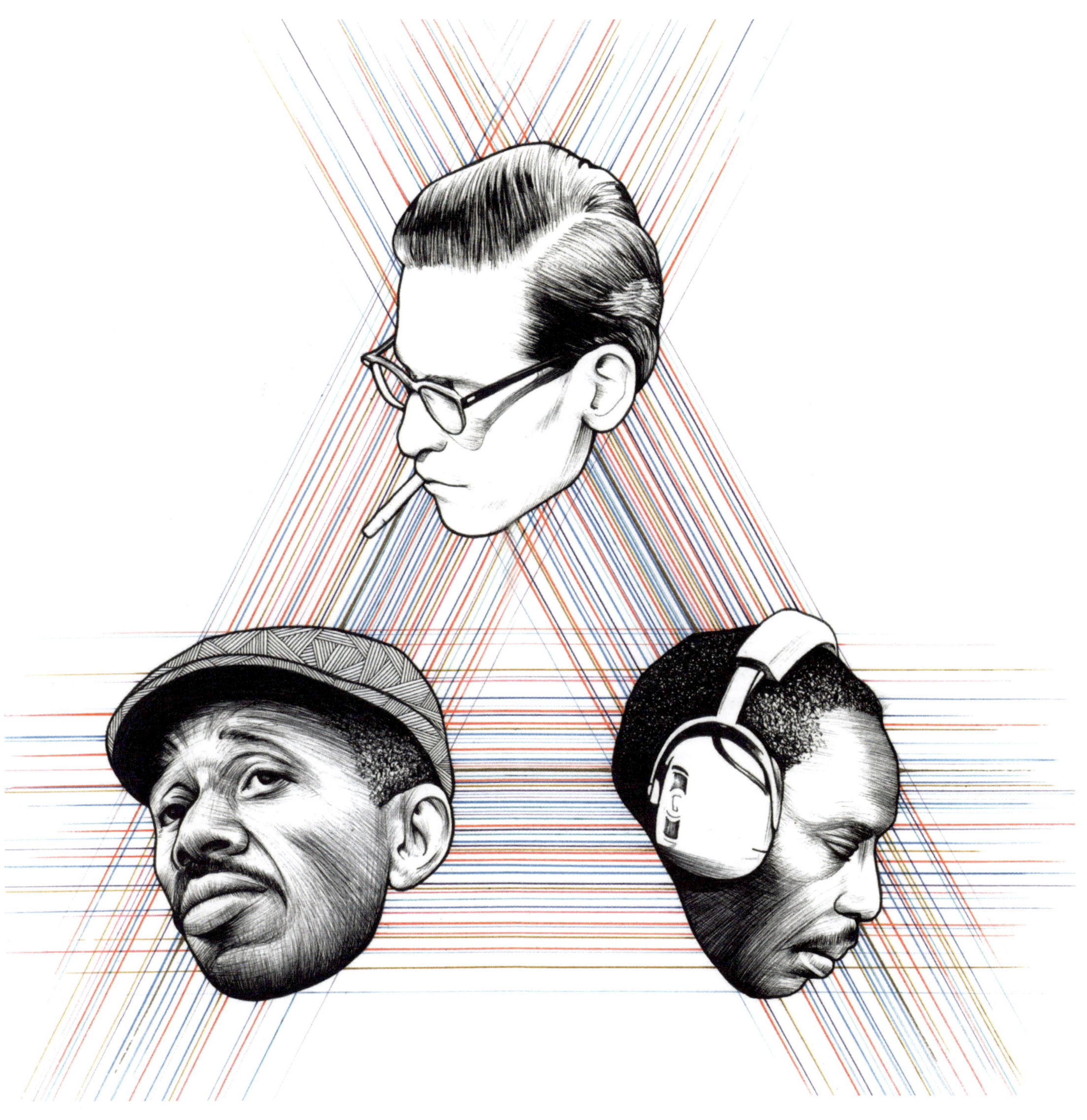

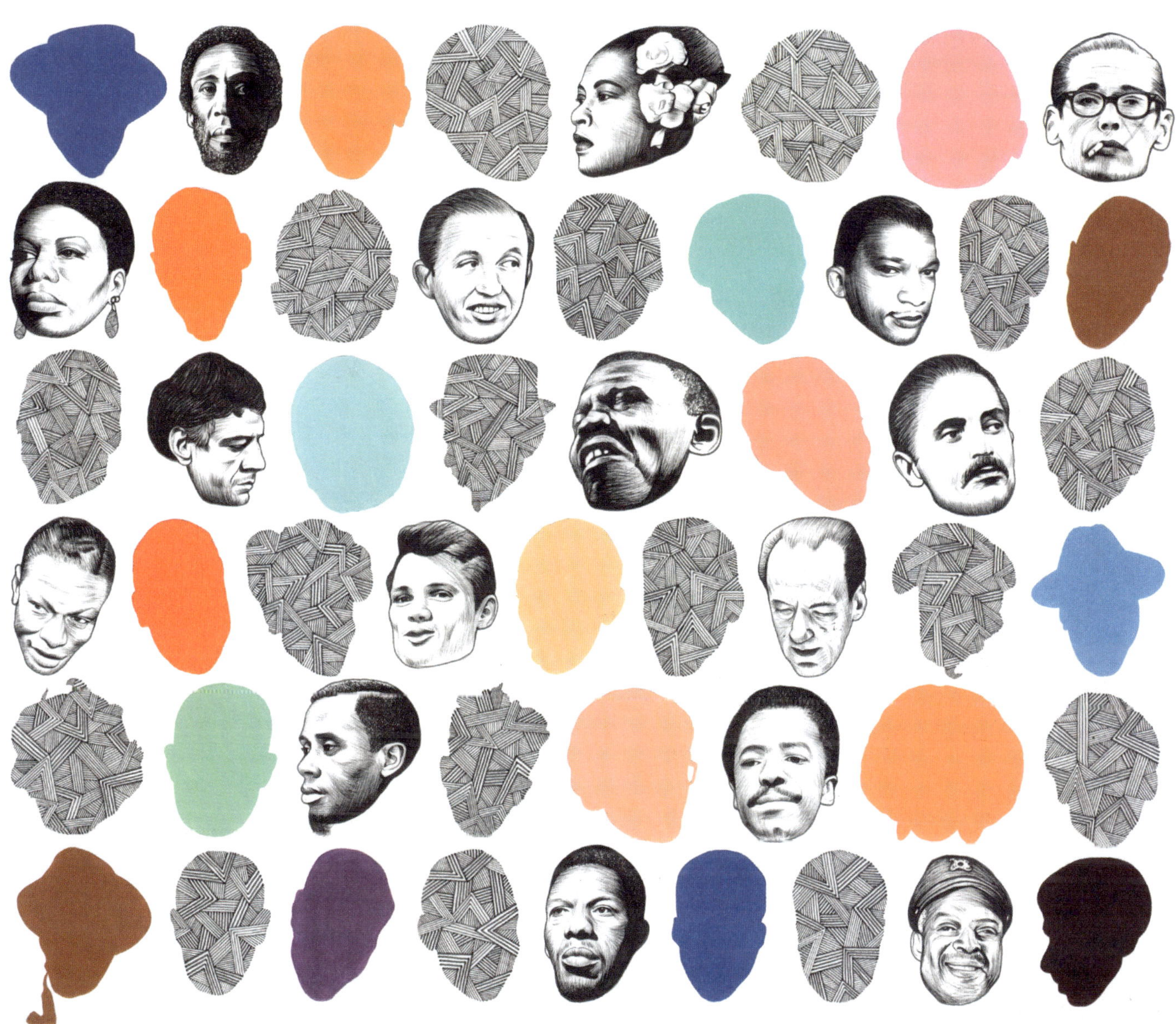

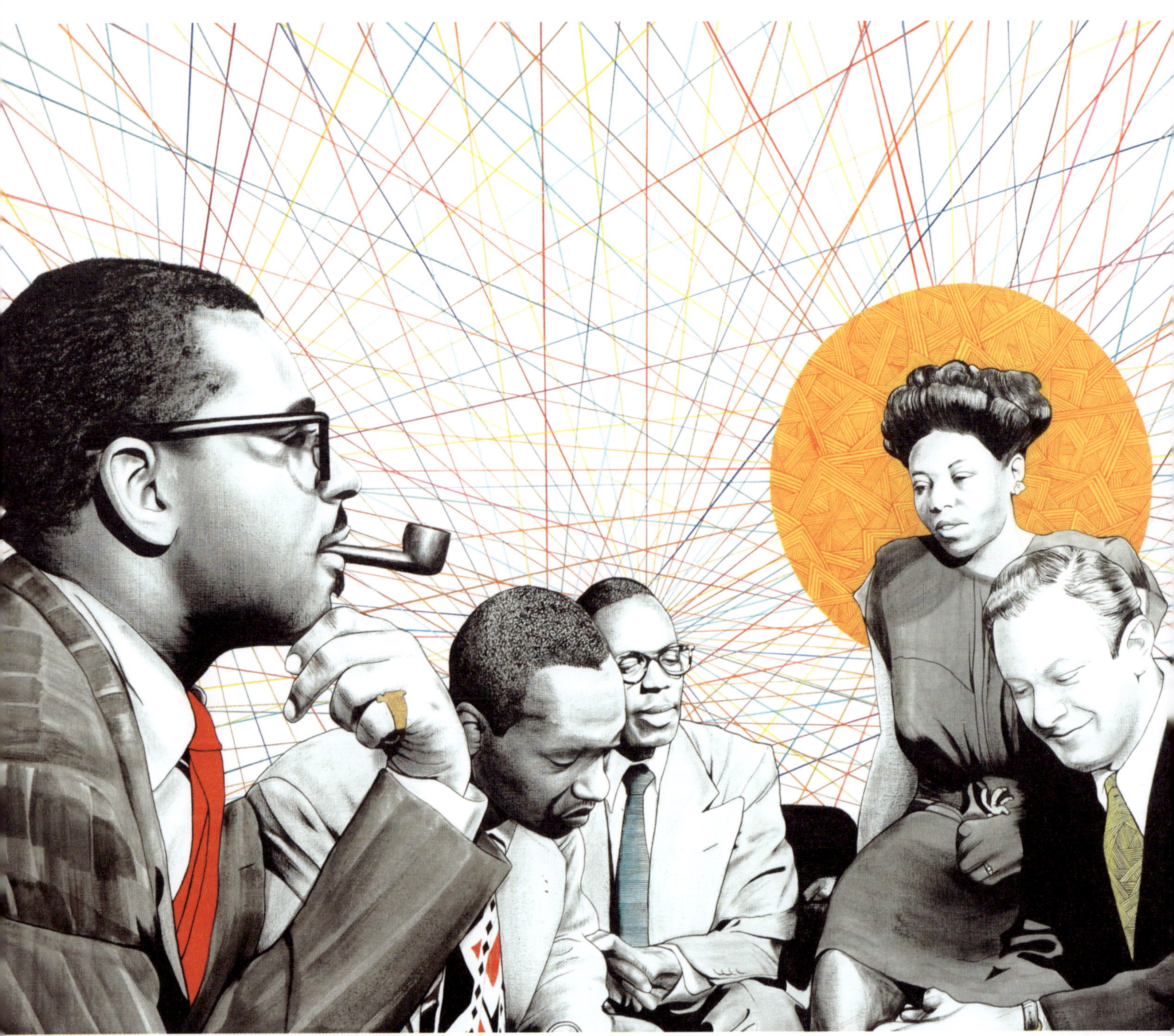

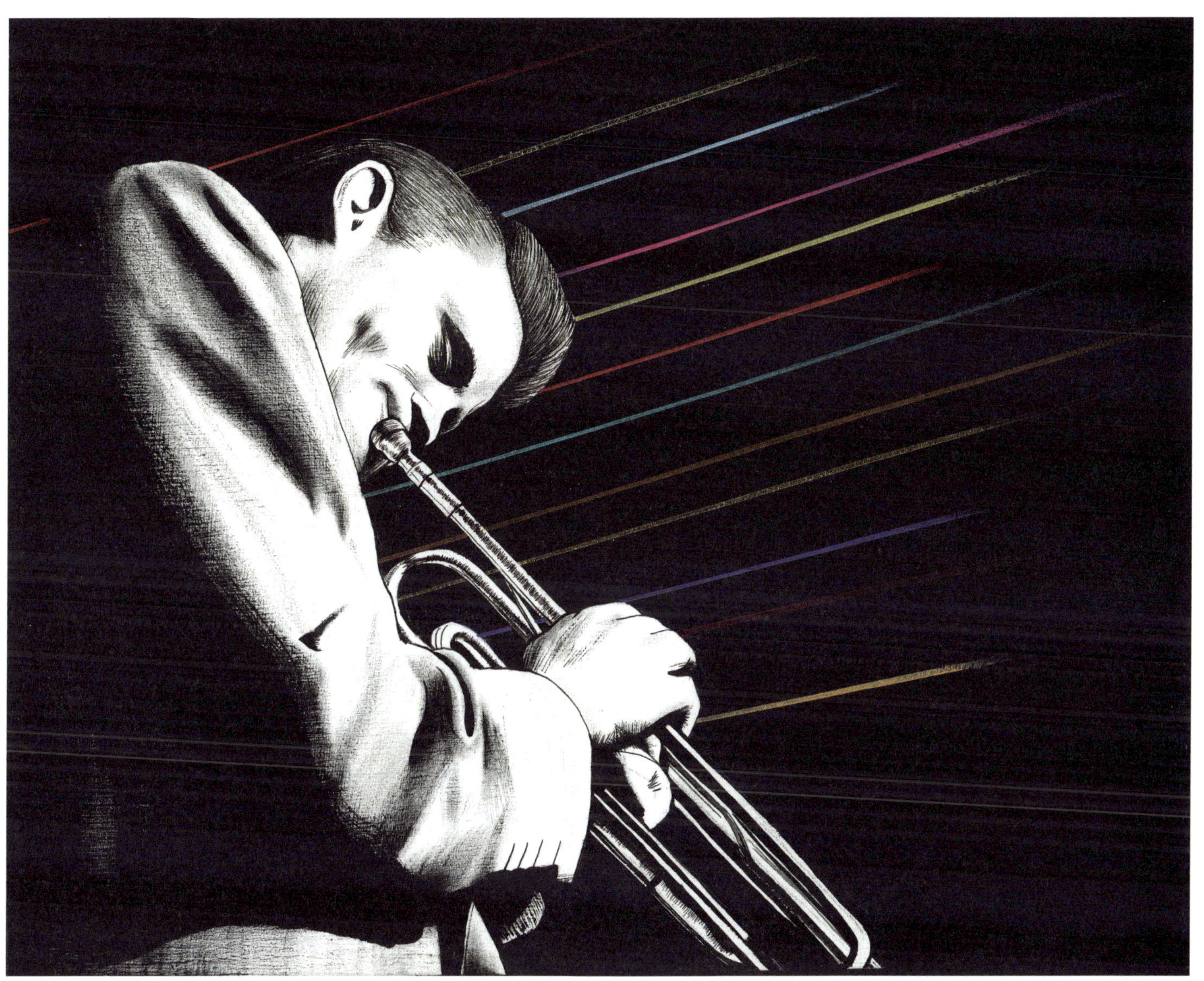

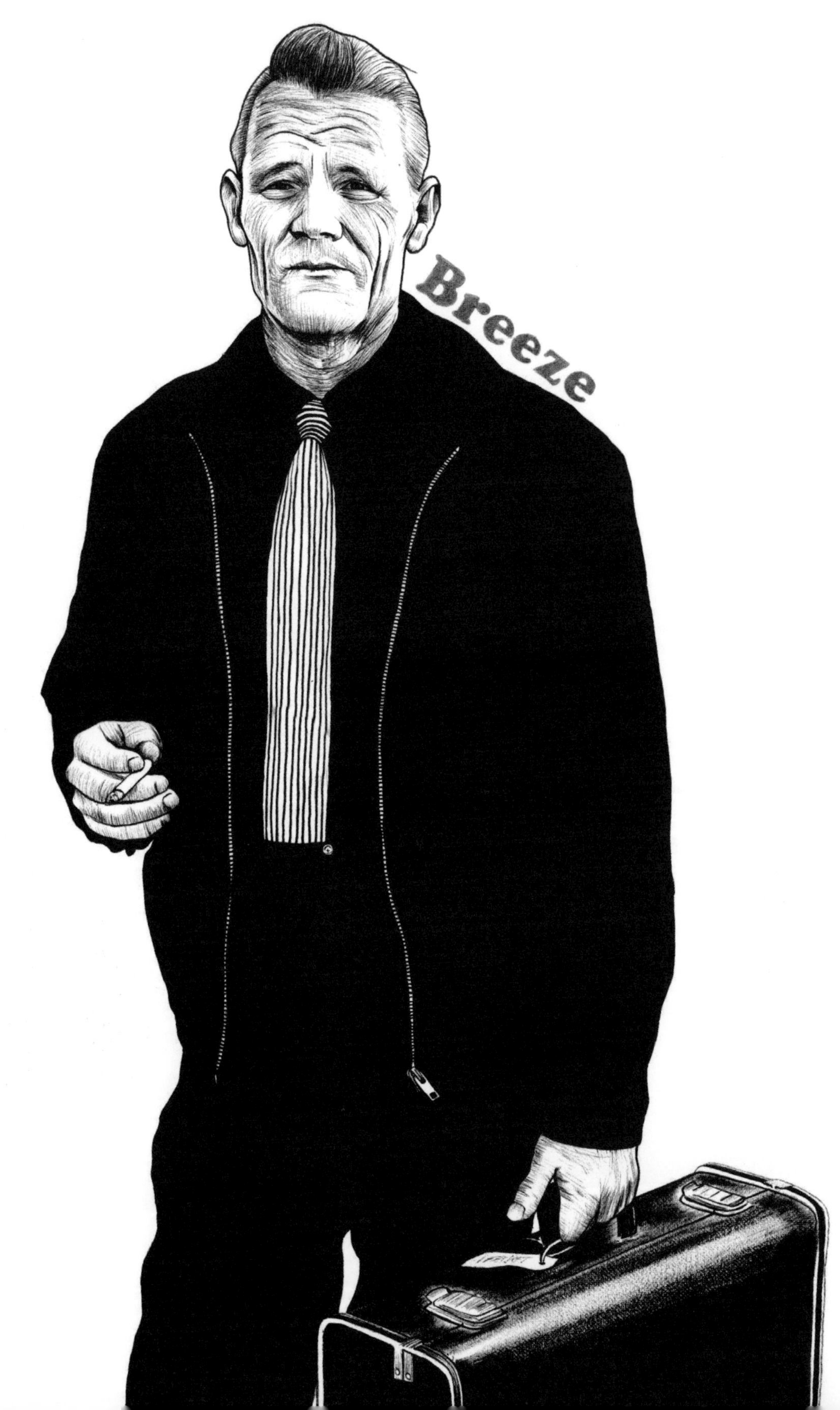
Breeze

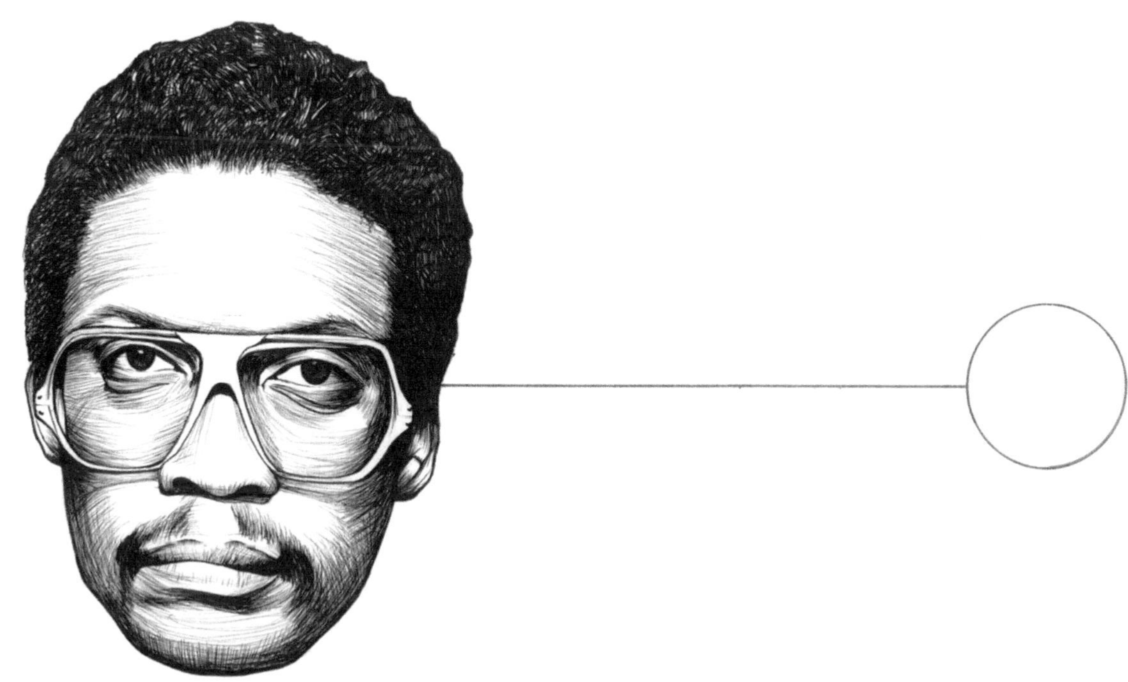

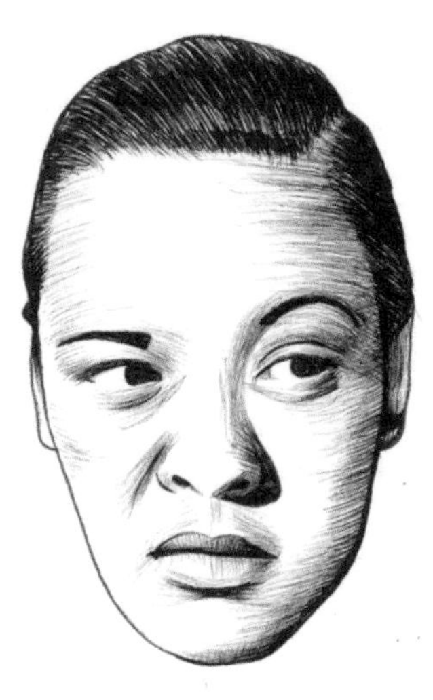

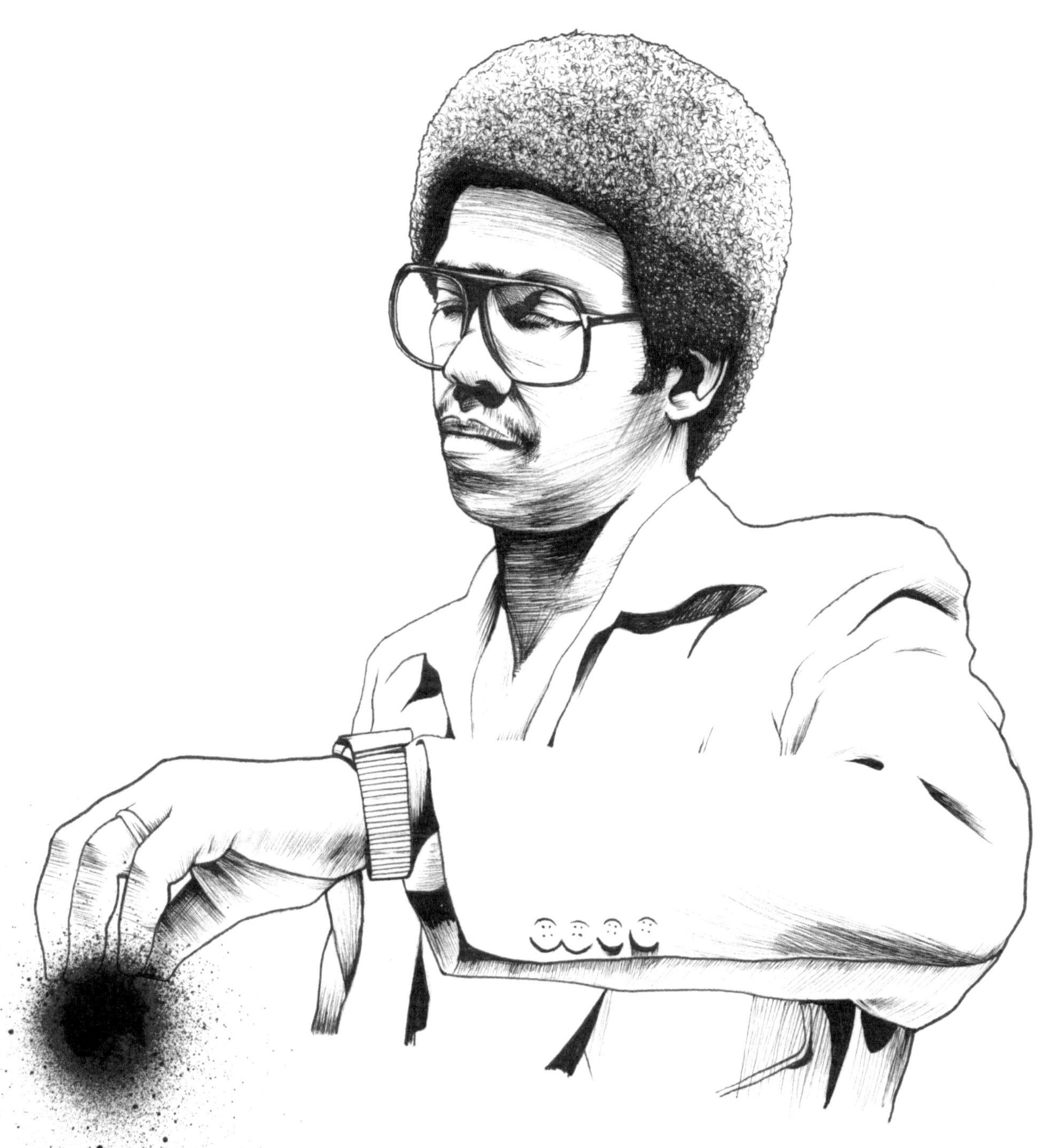

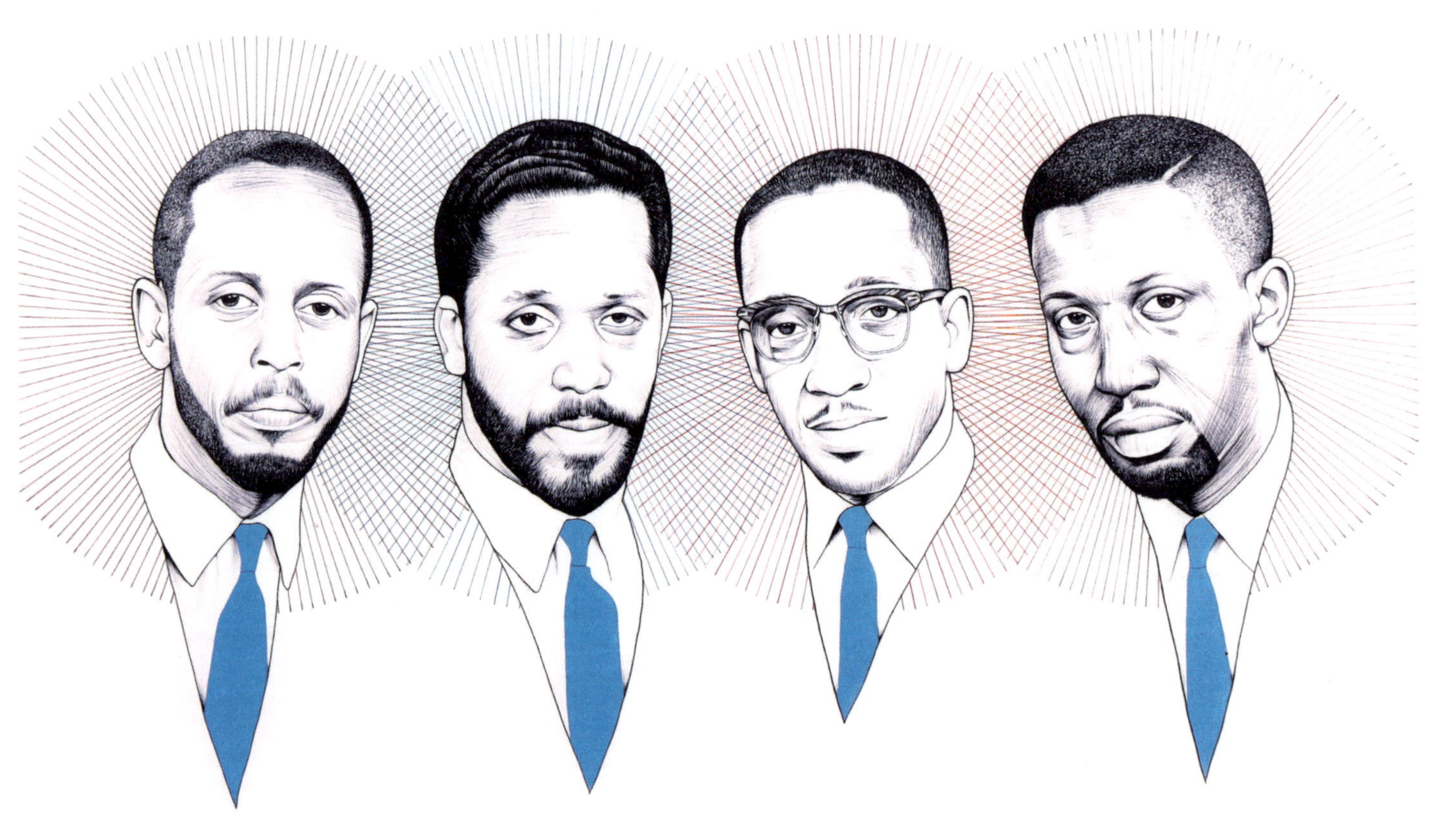

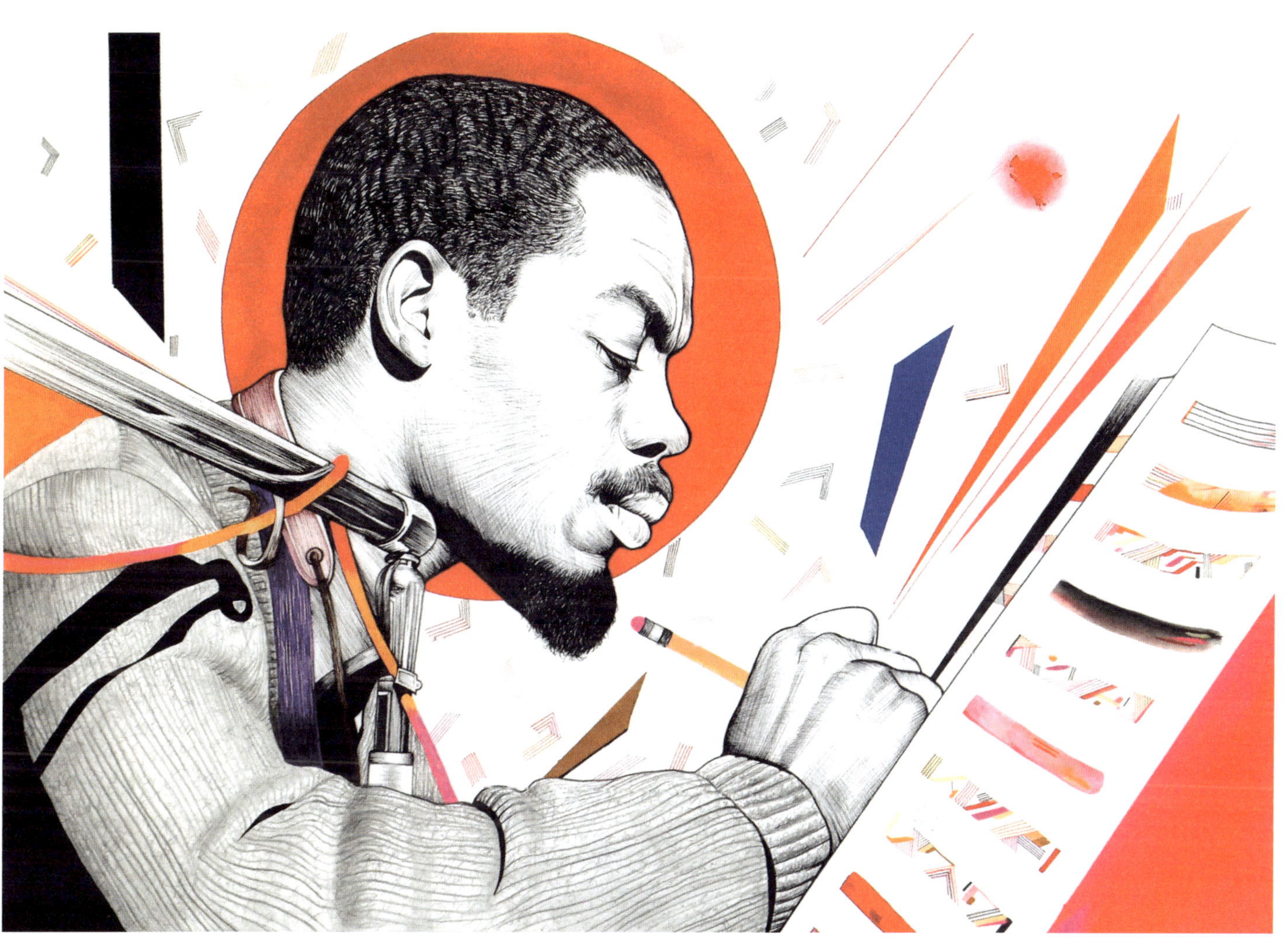

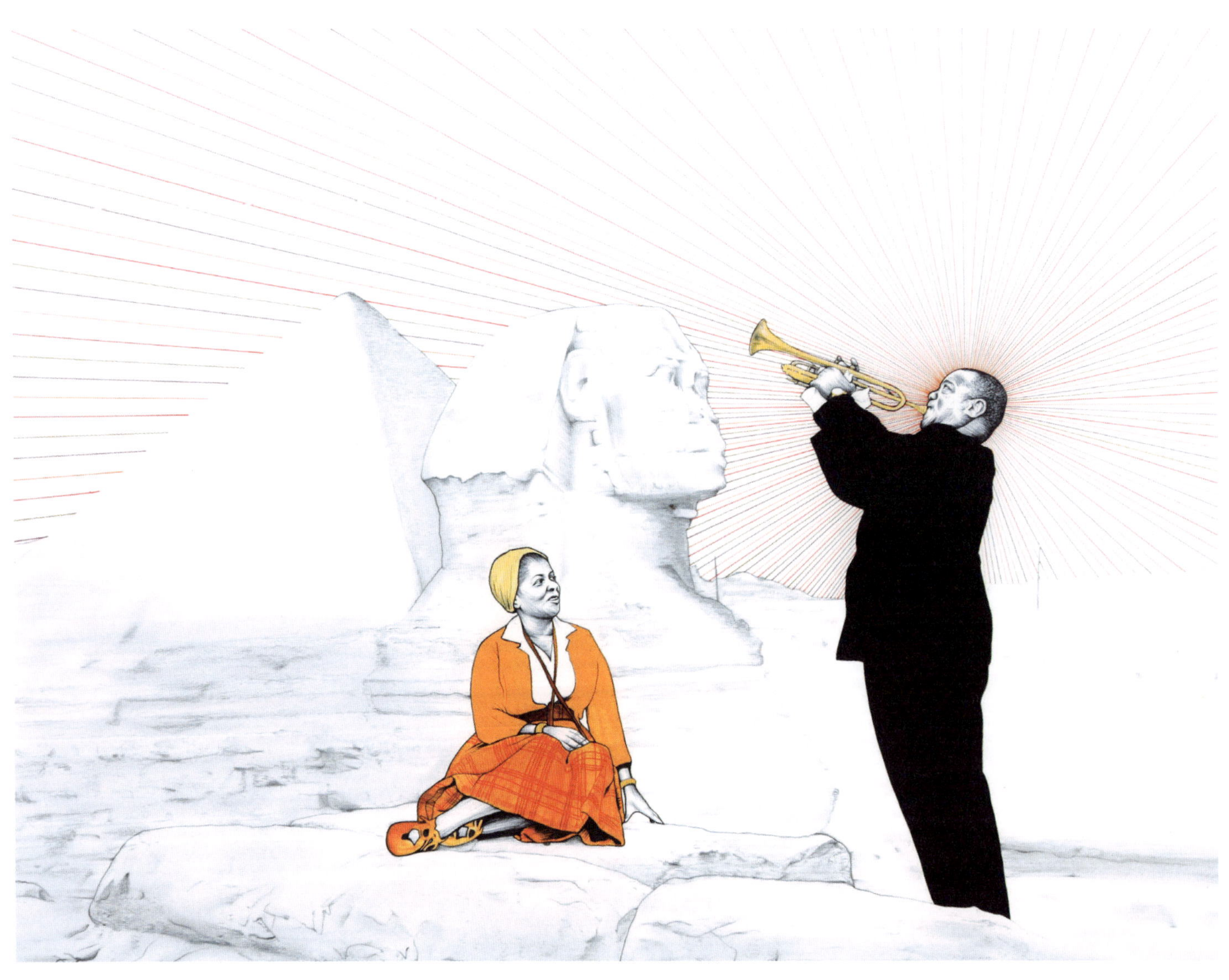

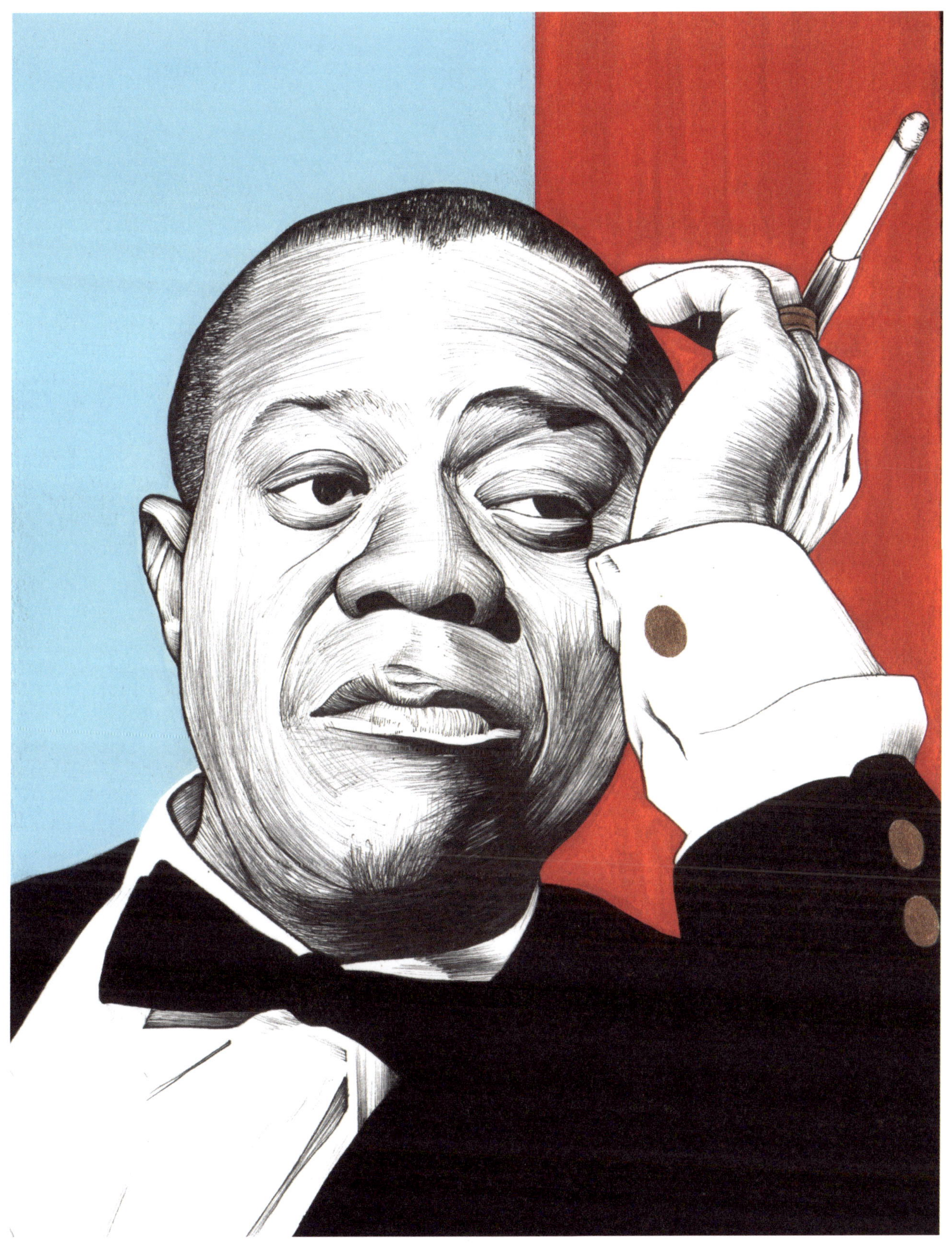

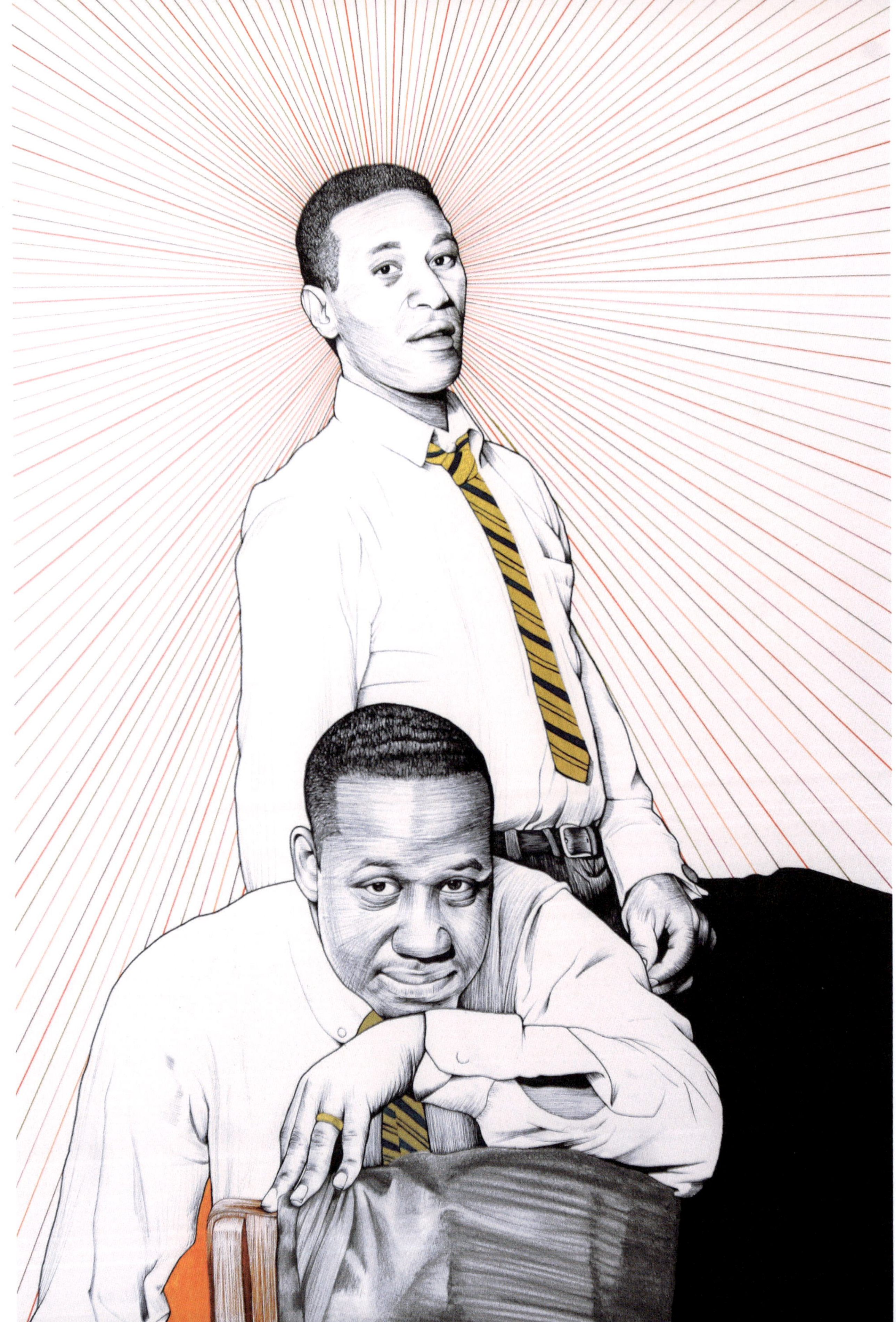

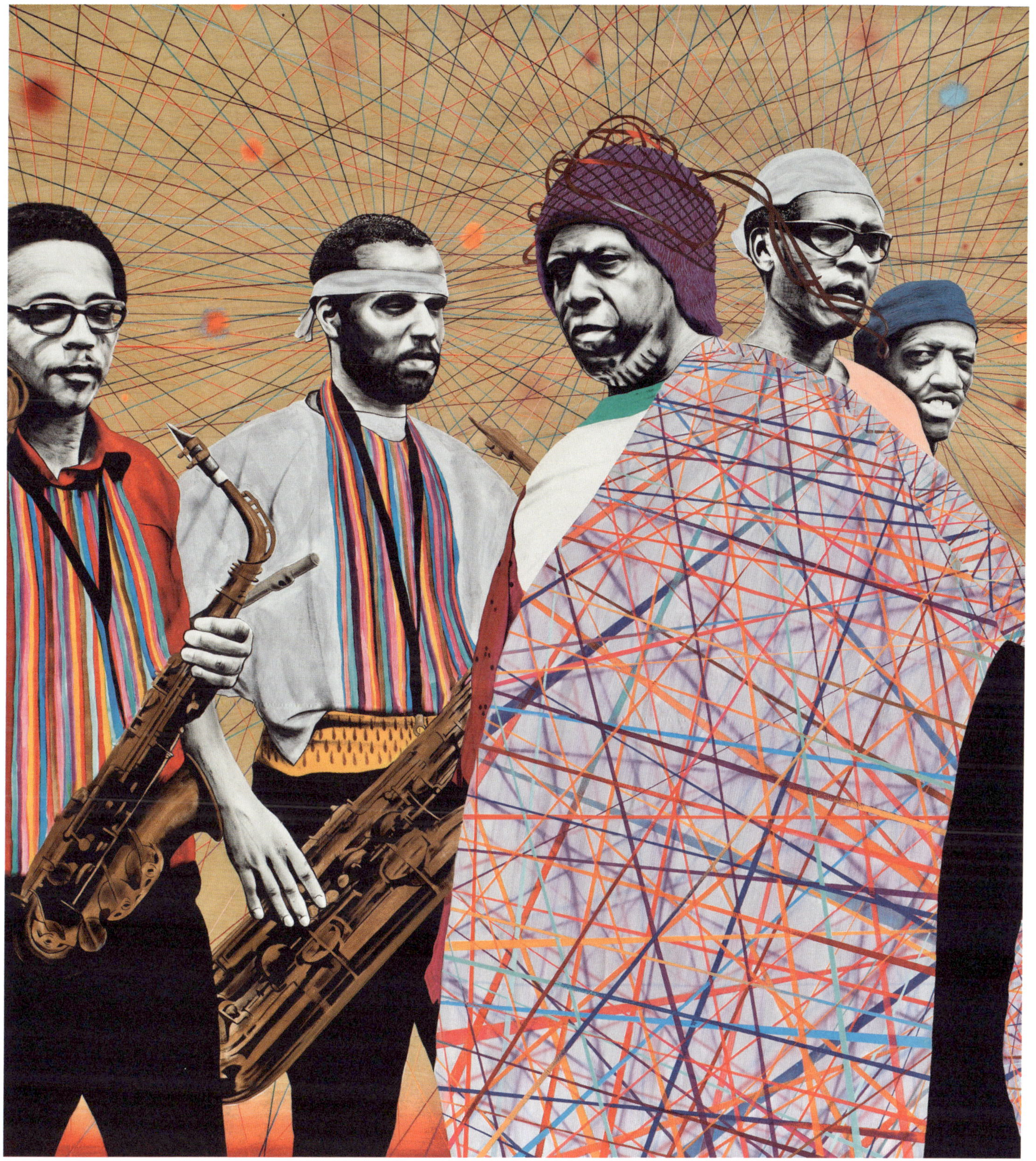

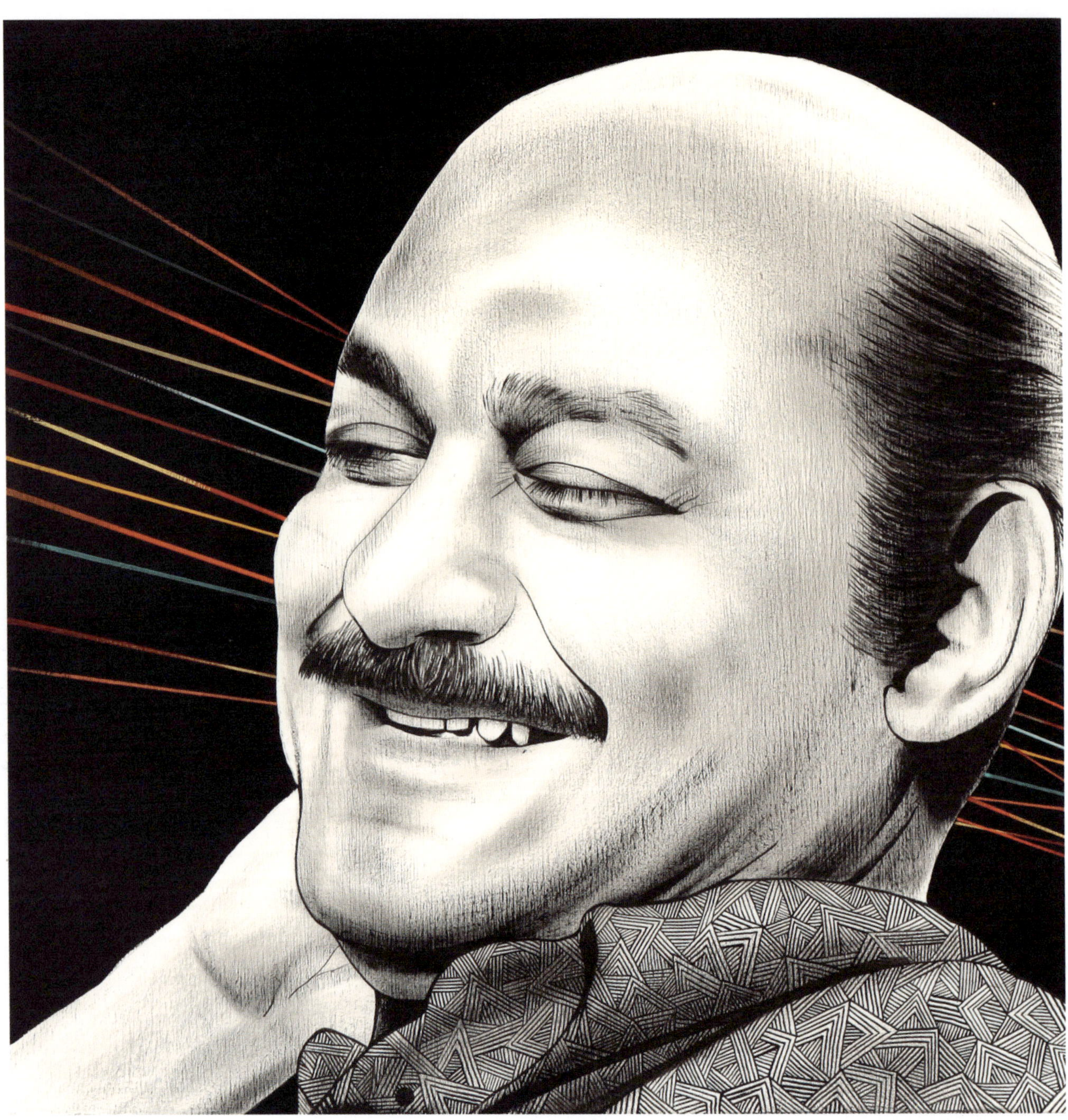

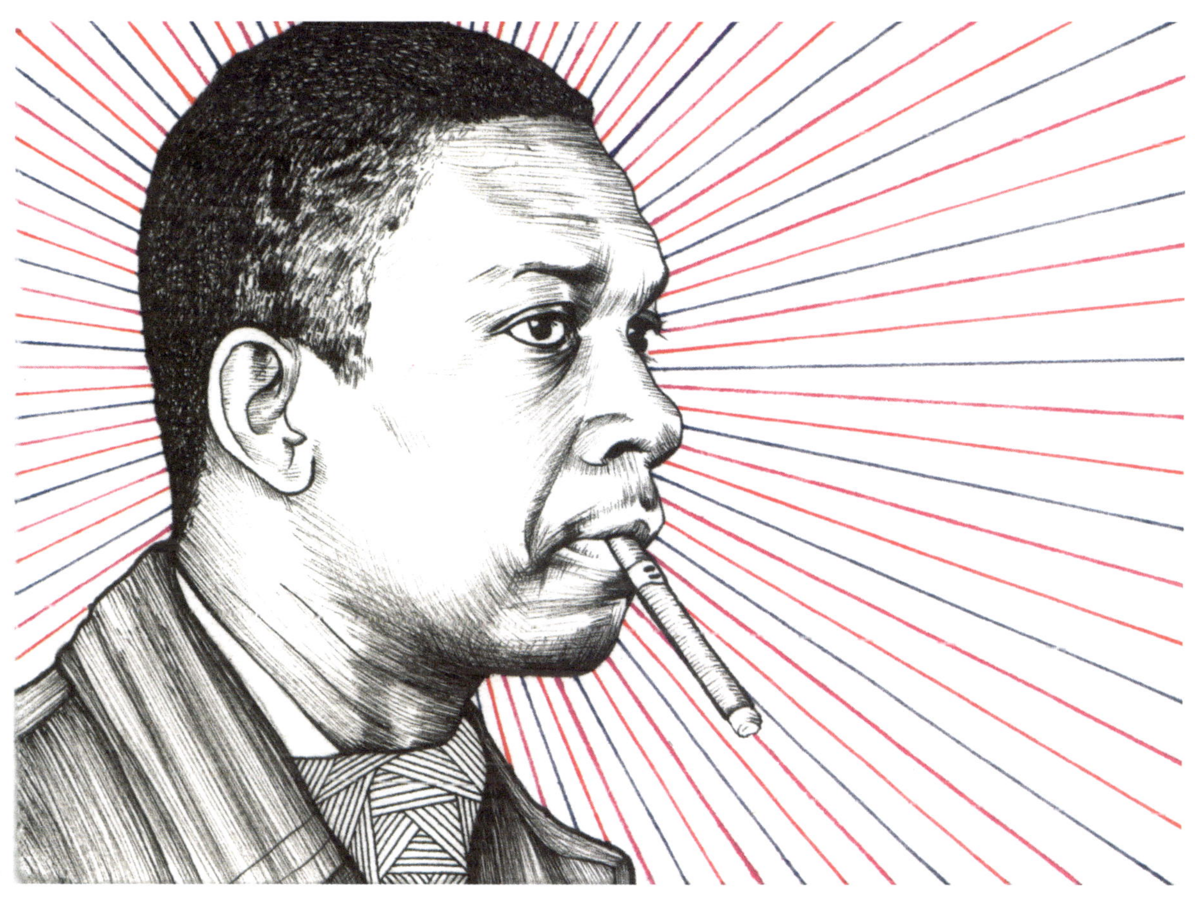

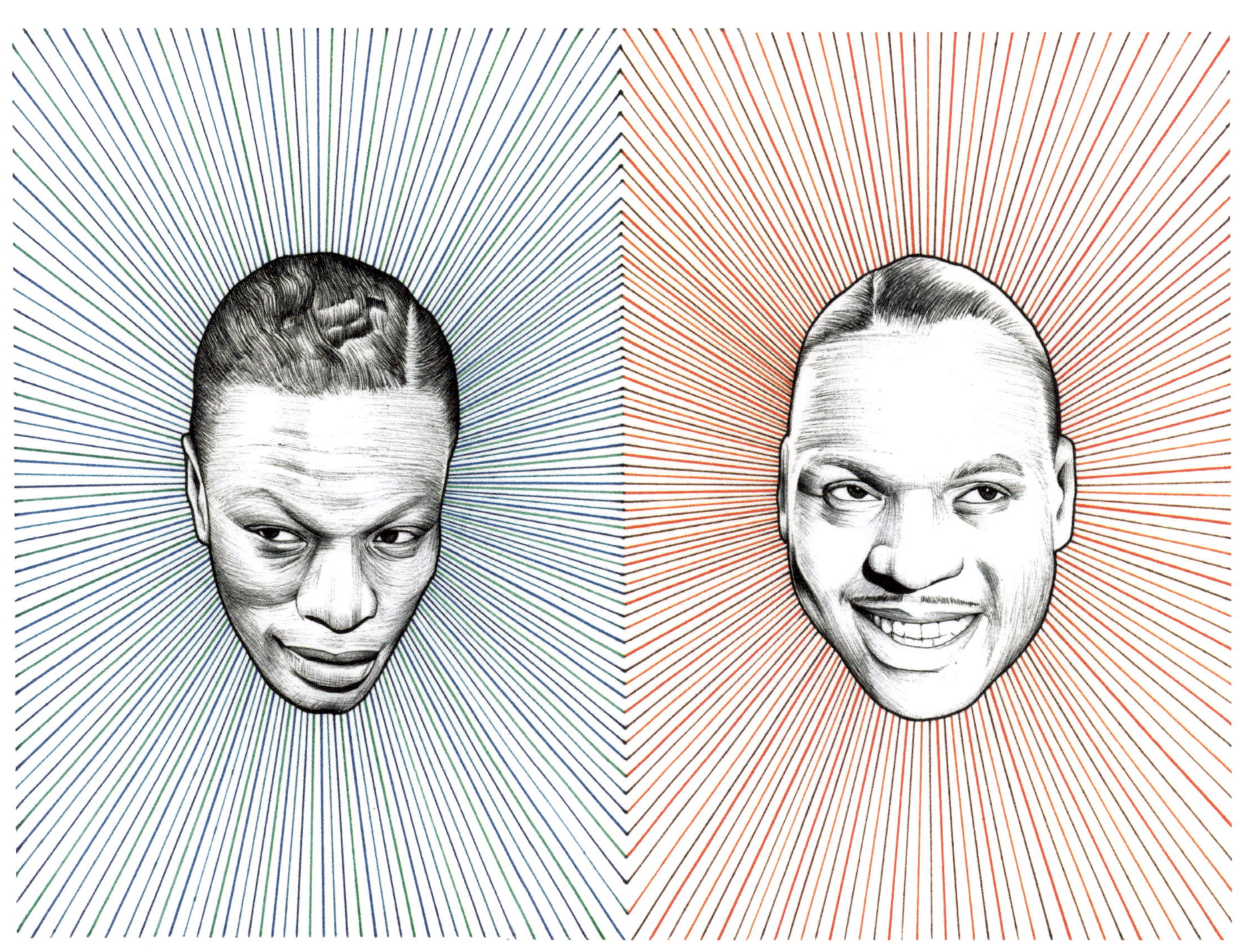

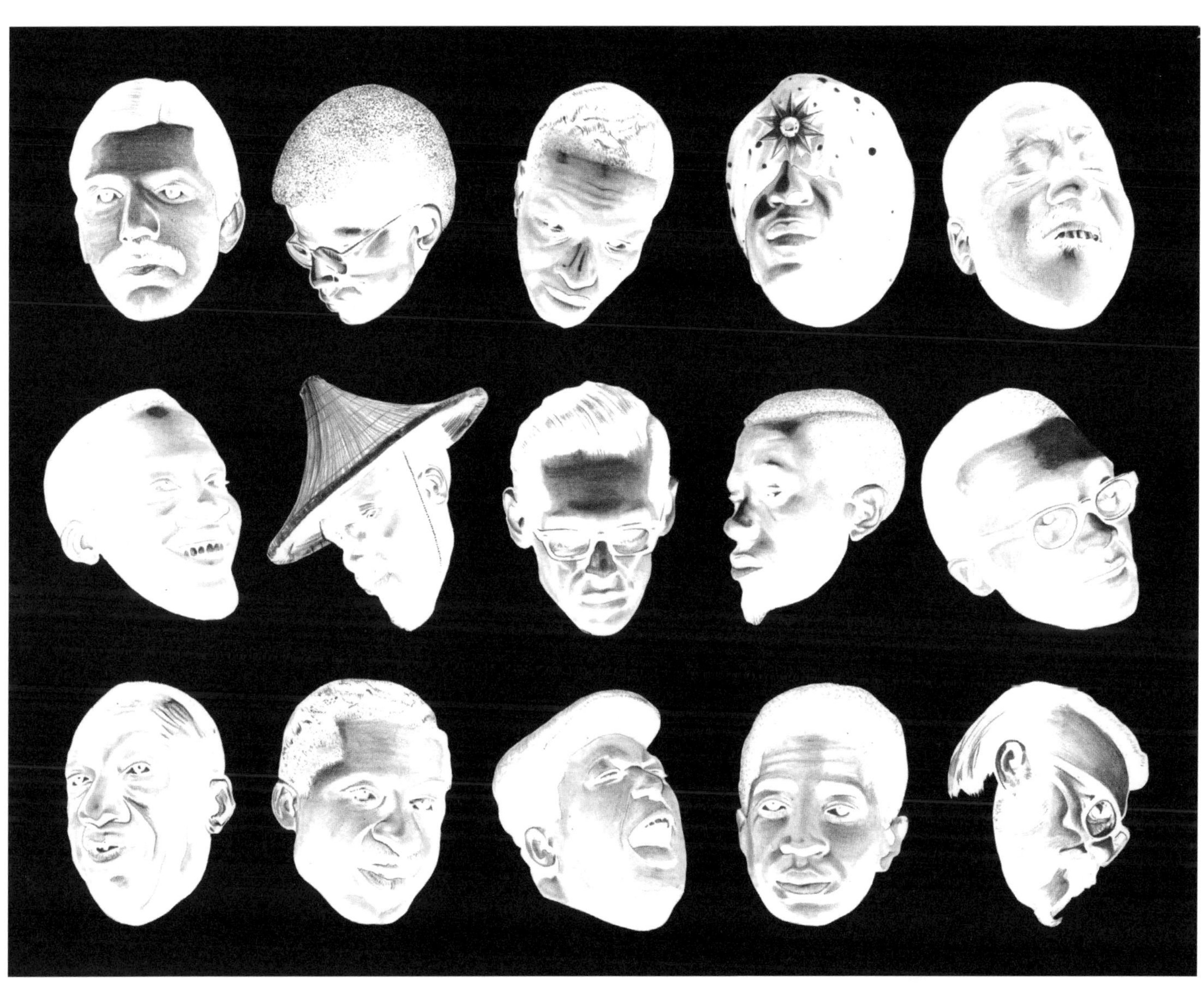

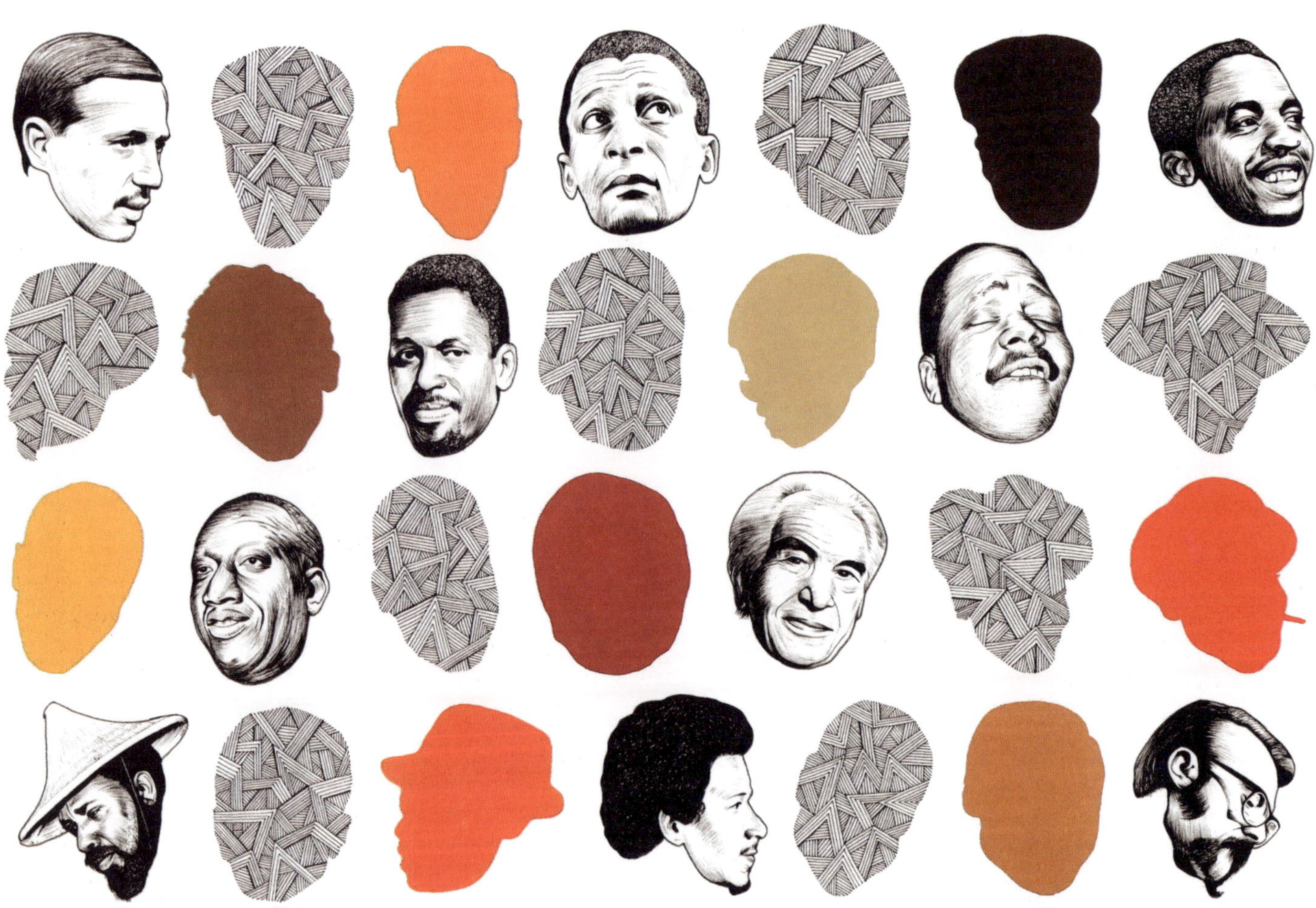

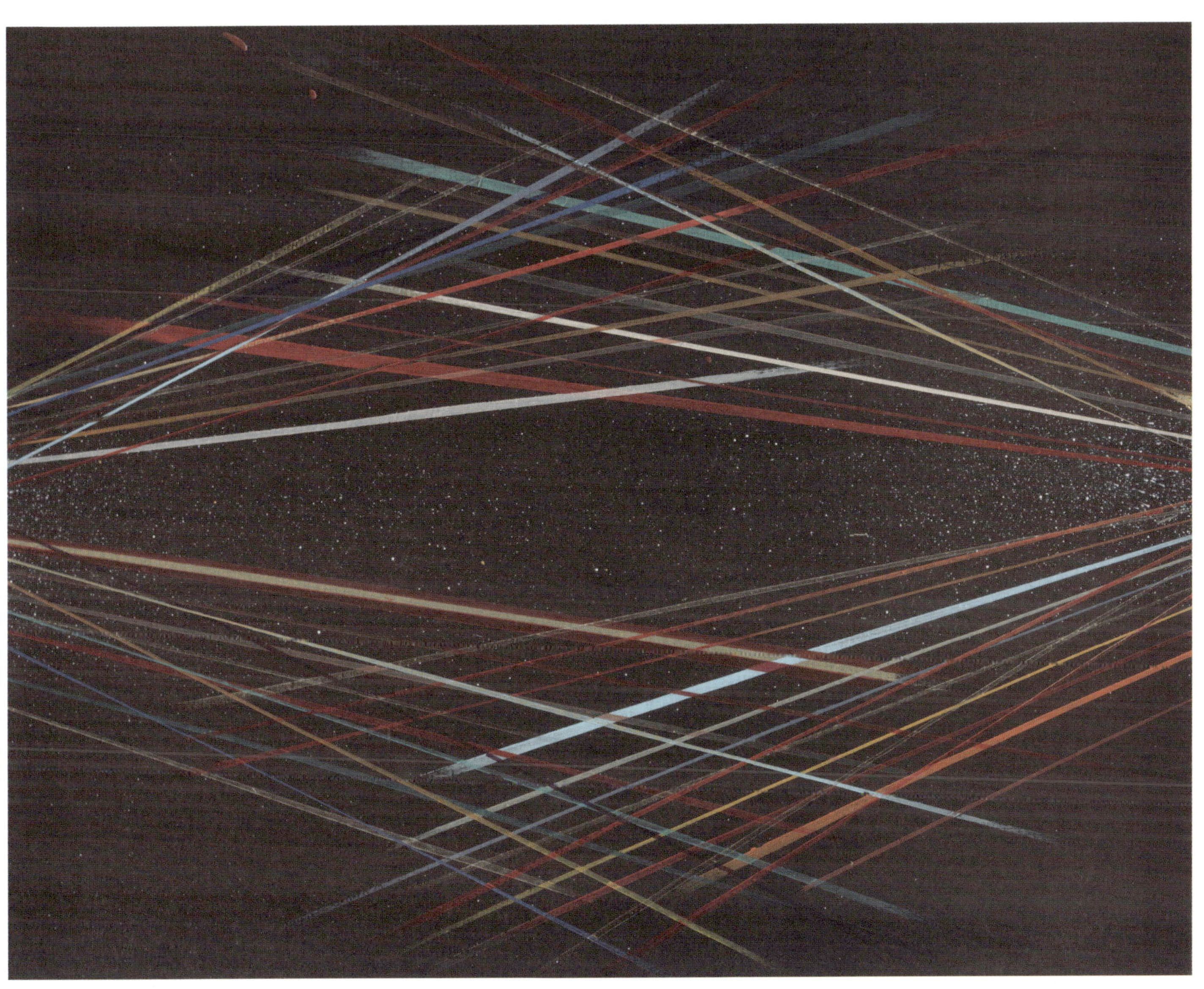

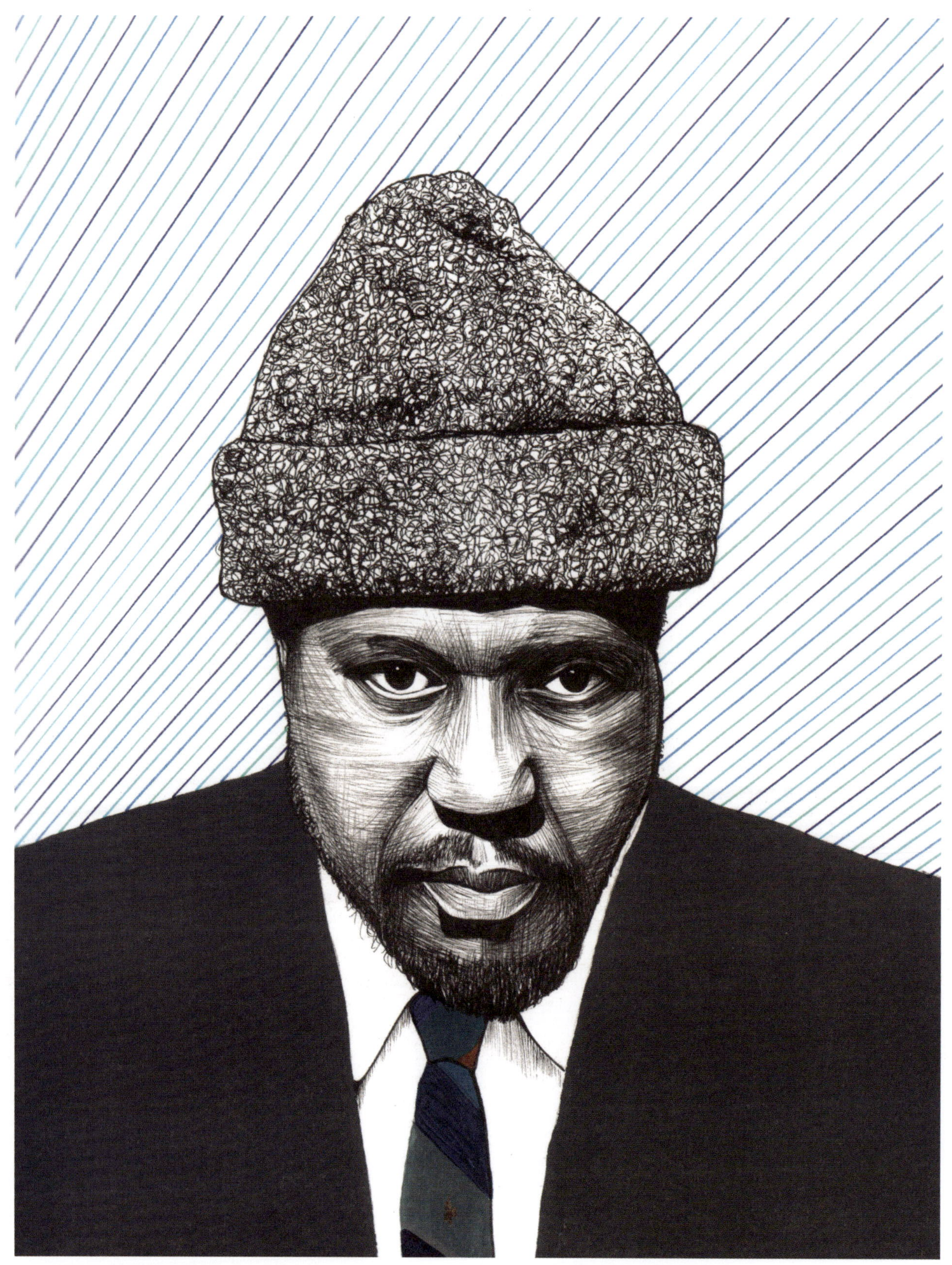

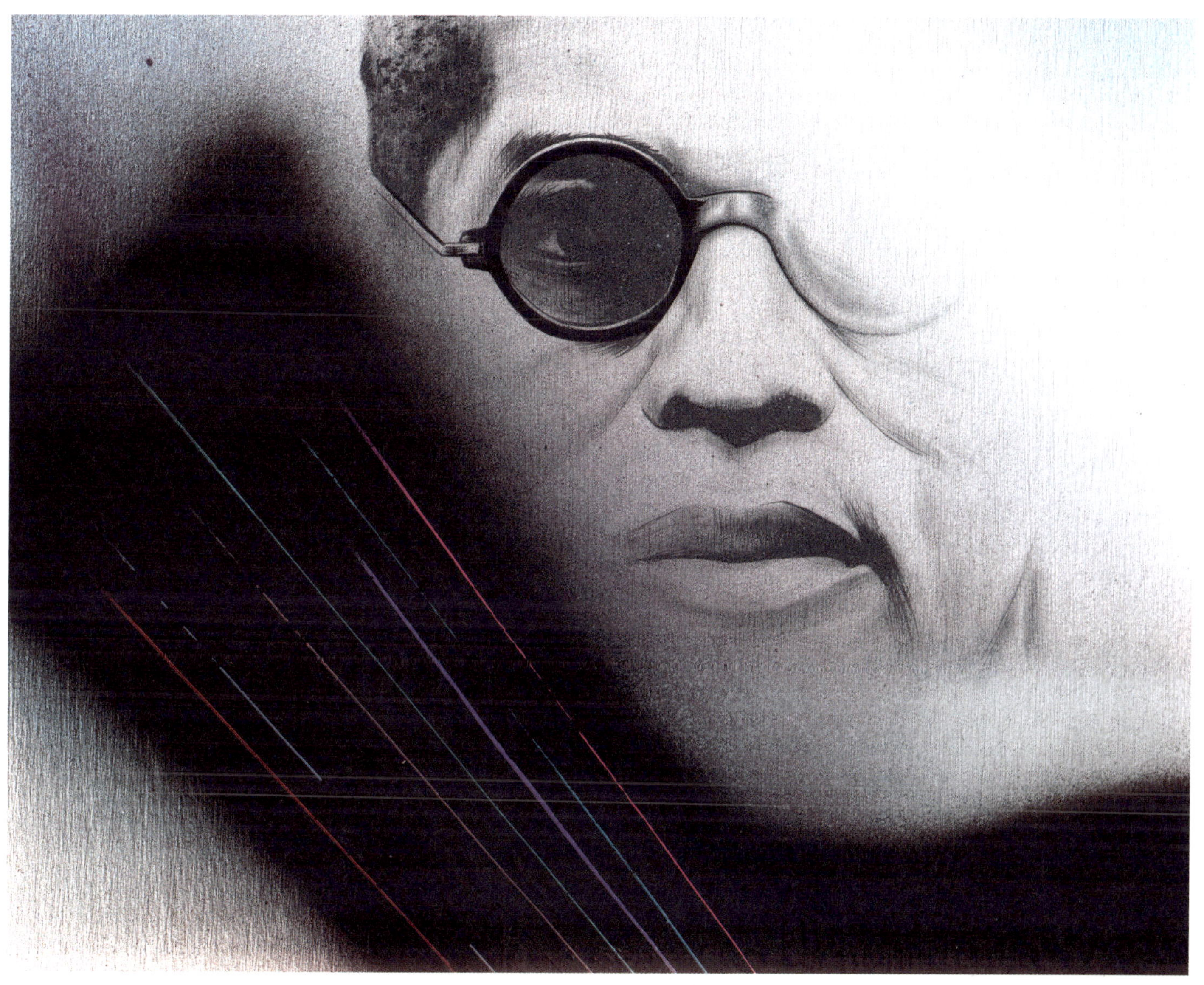

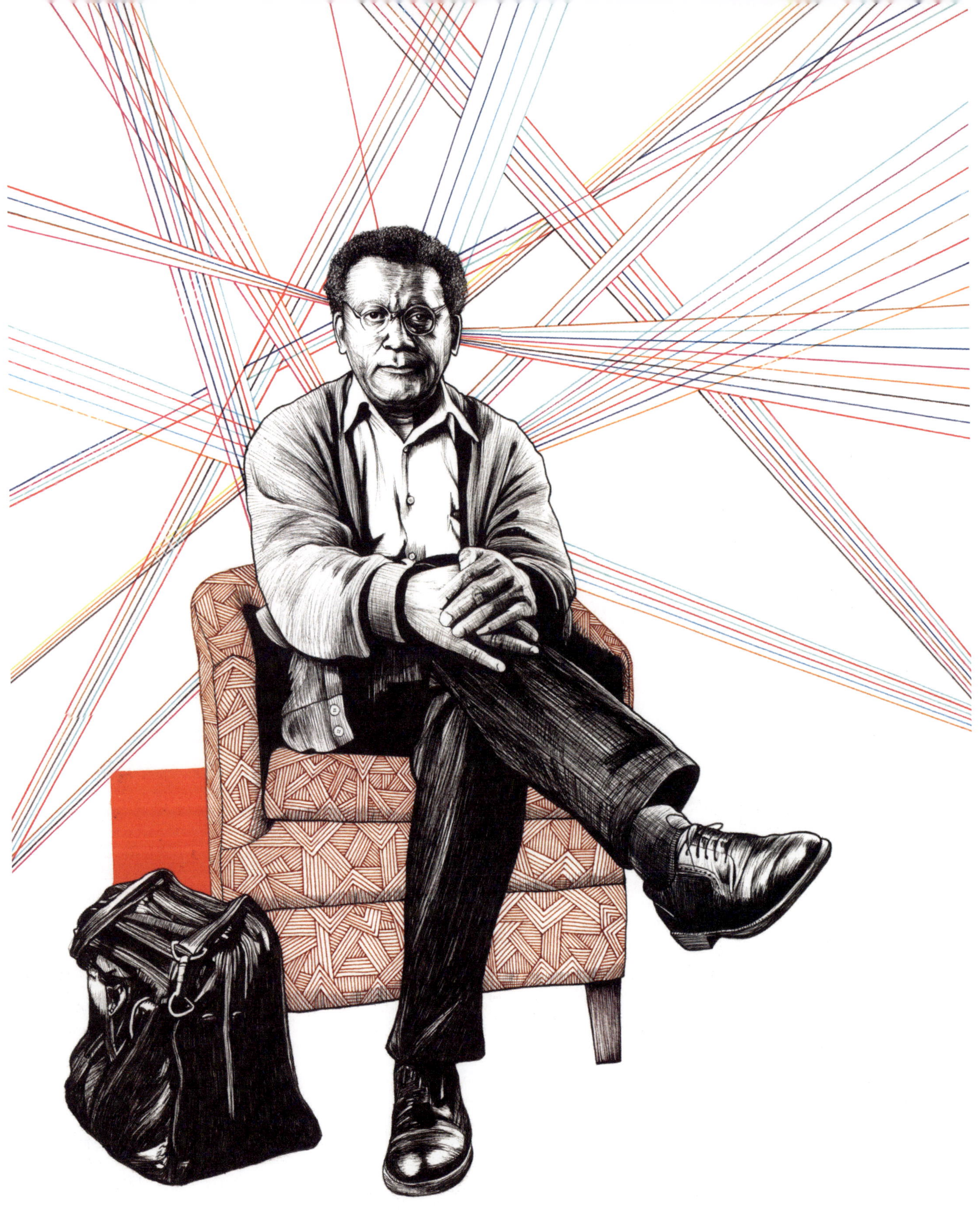

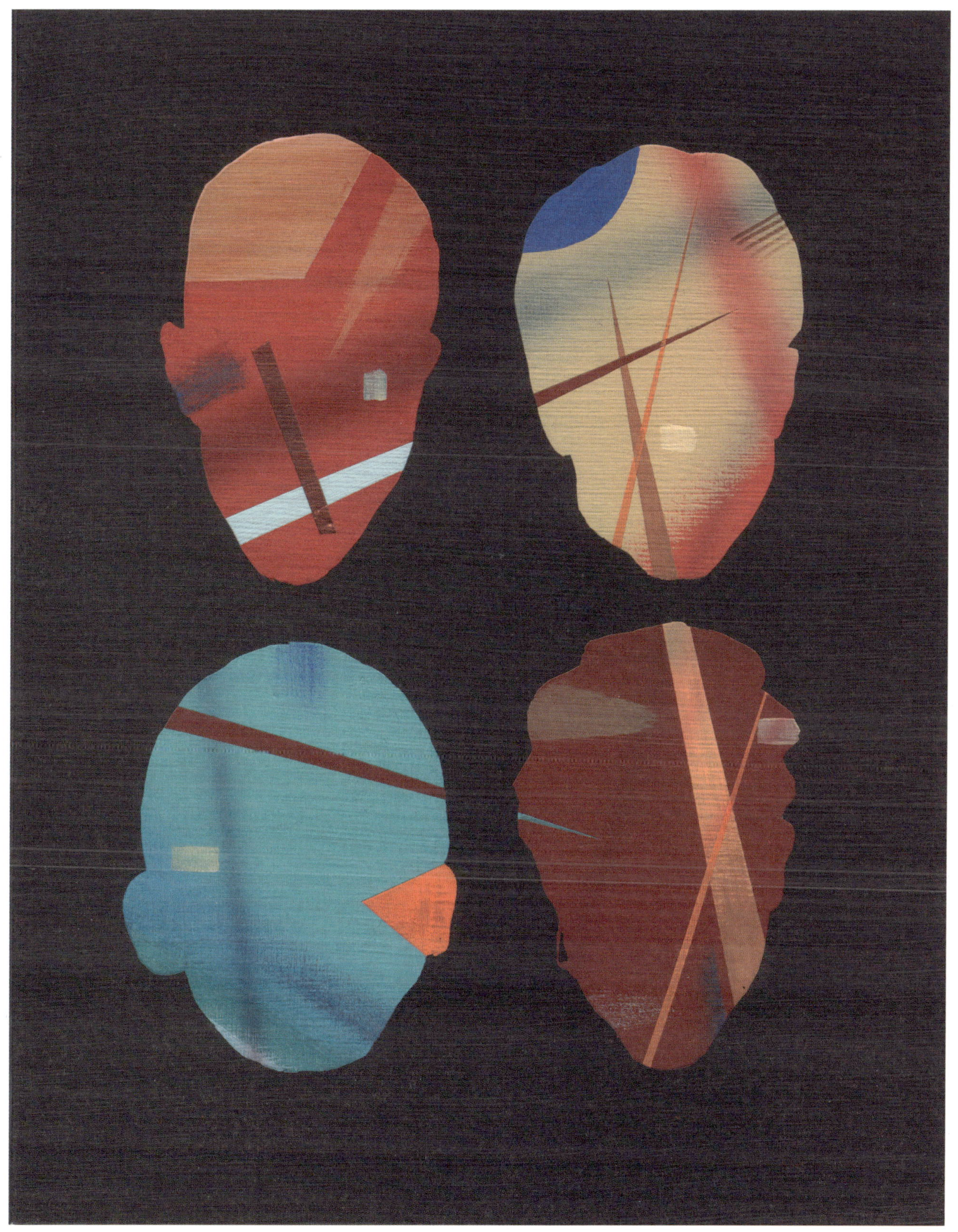

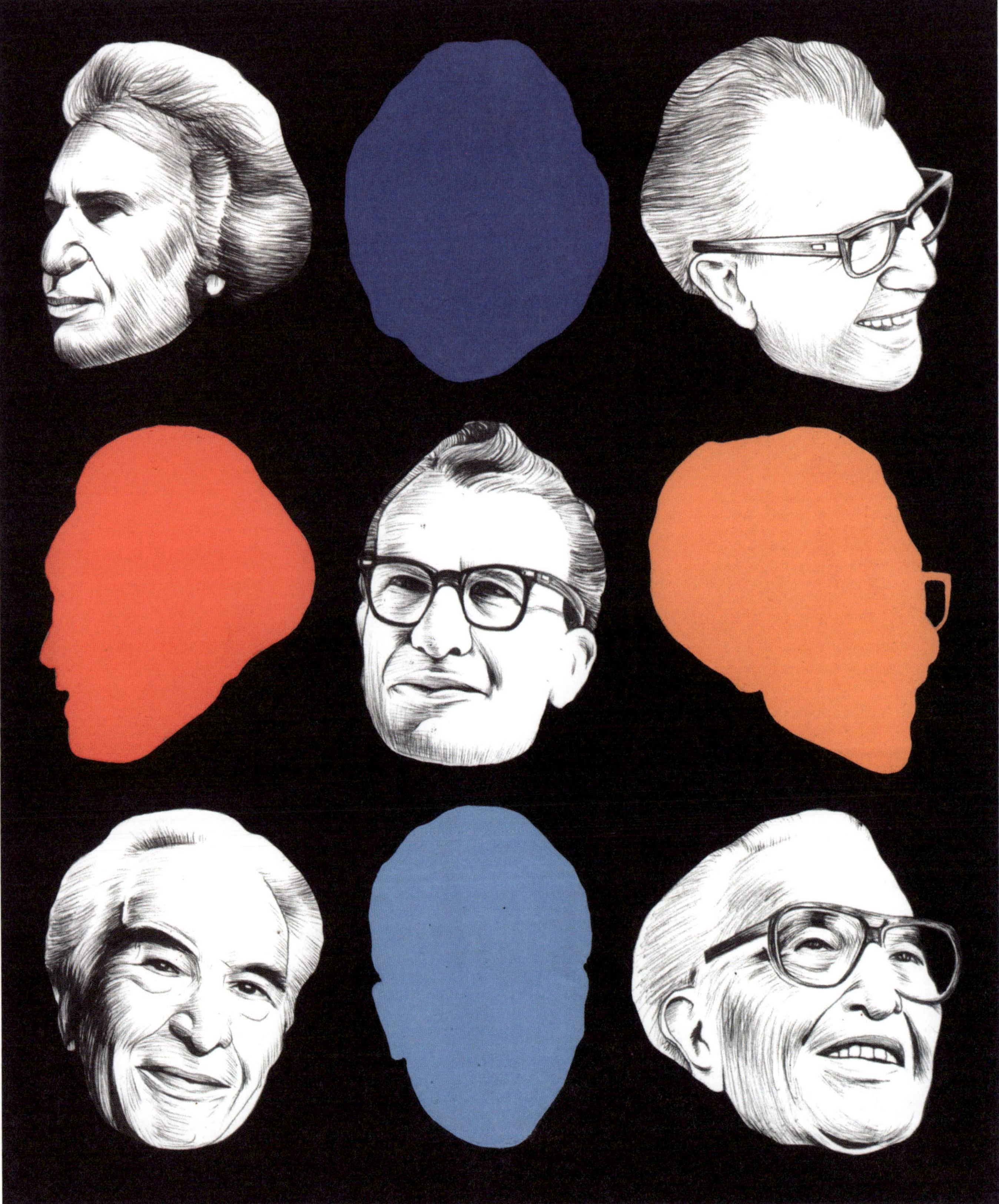

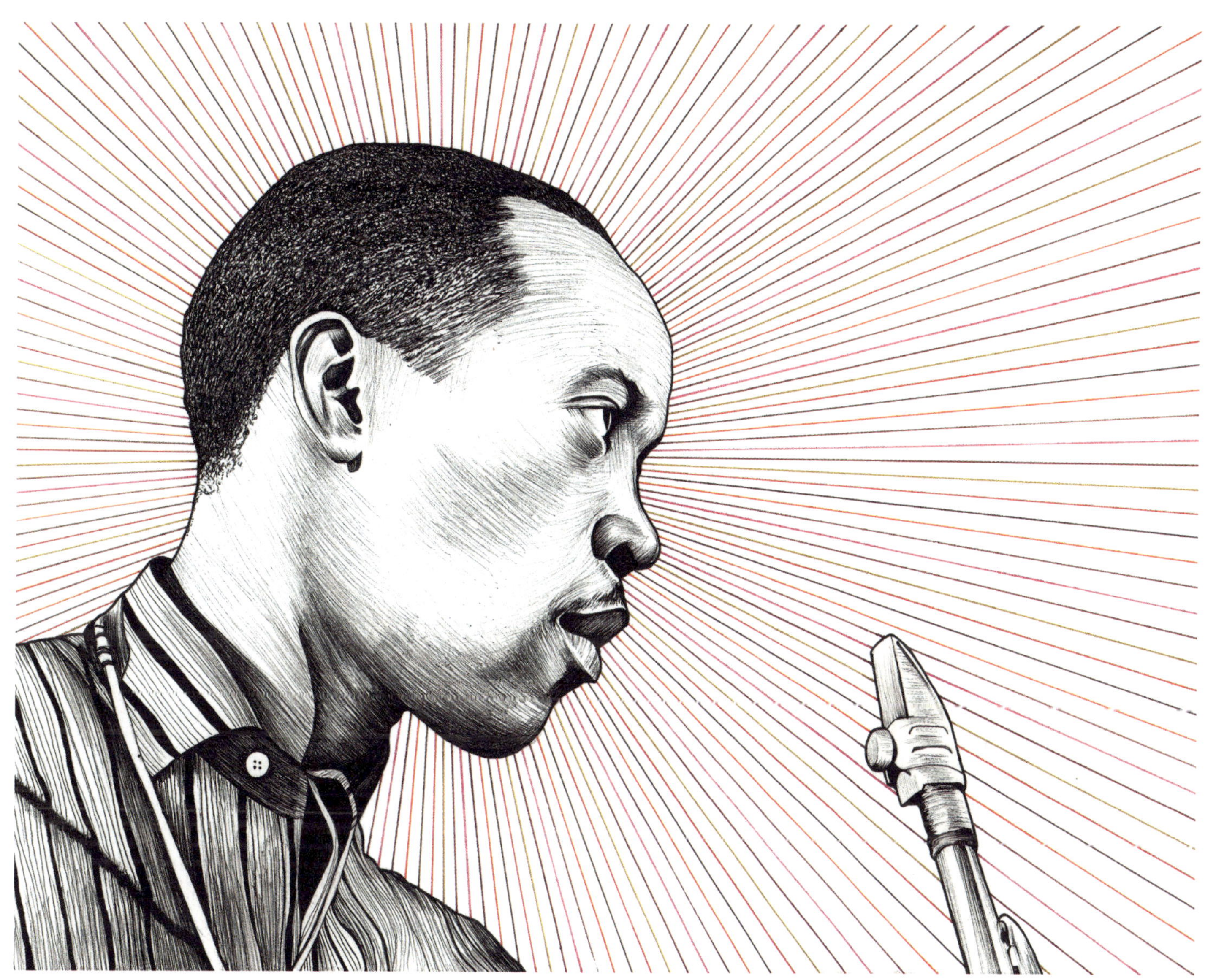

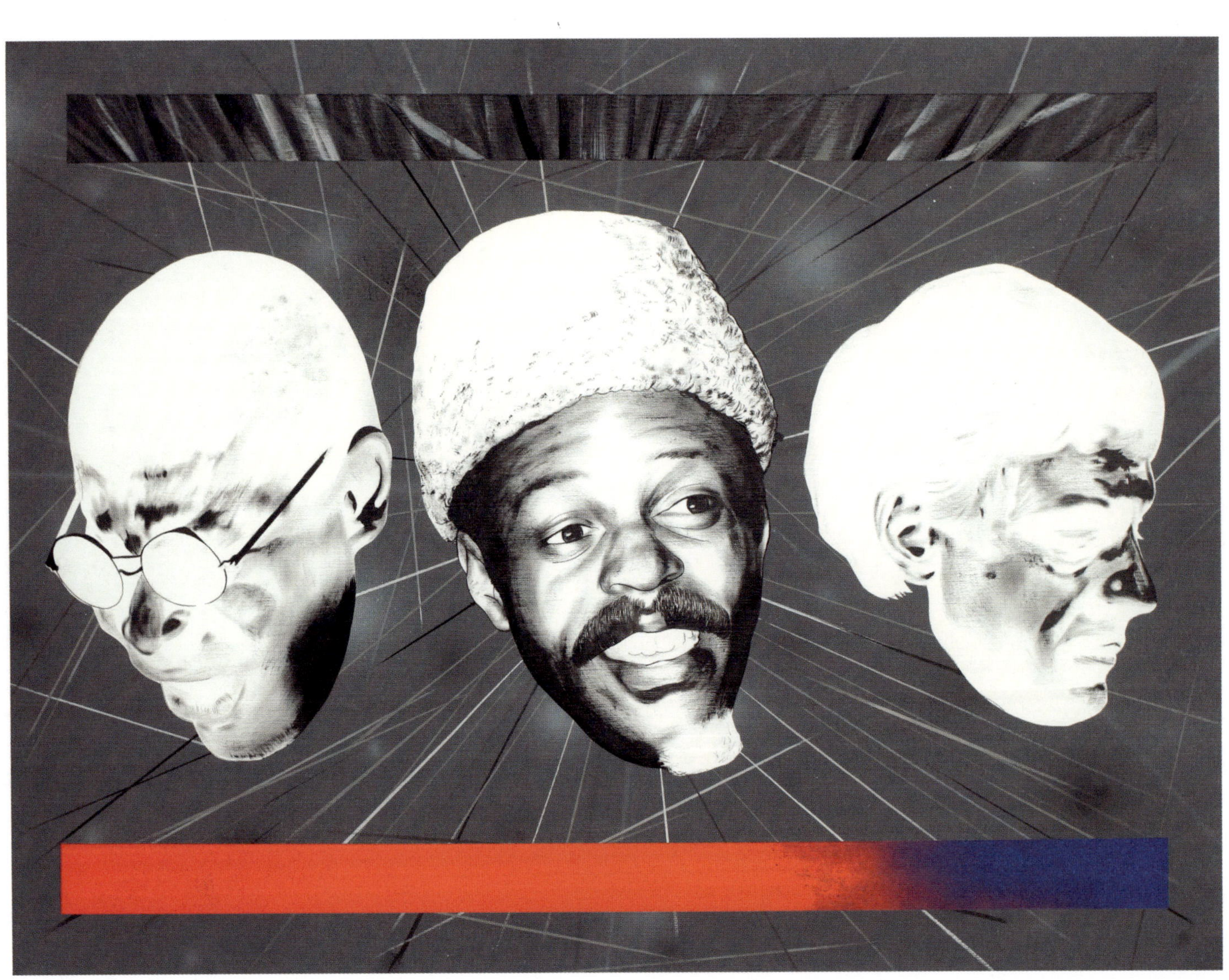

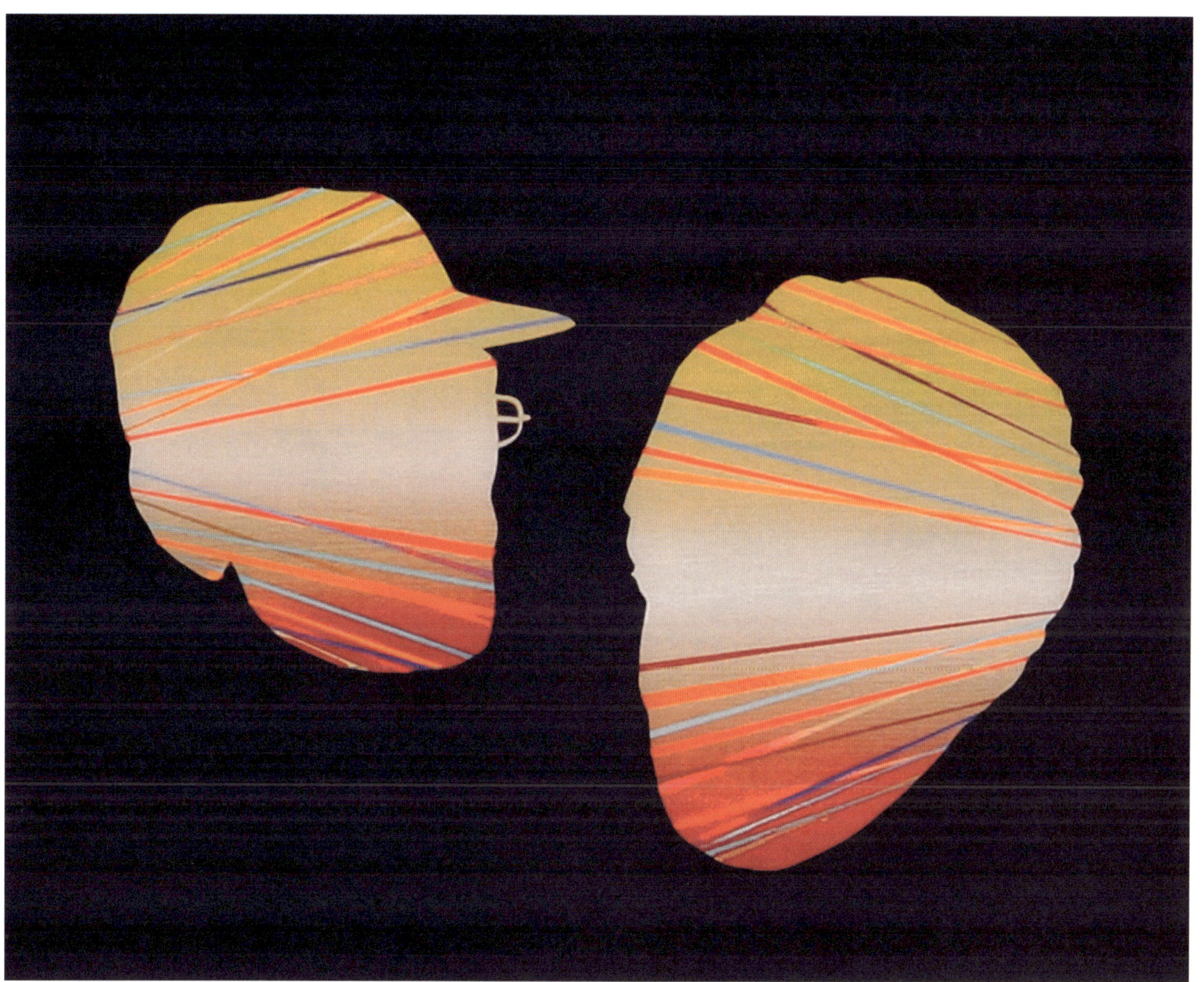

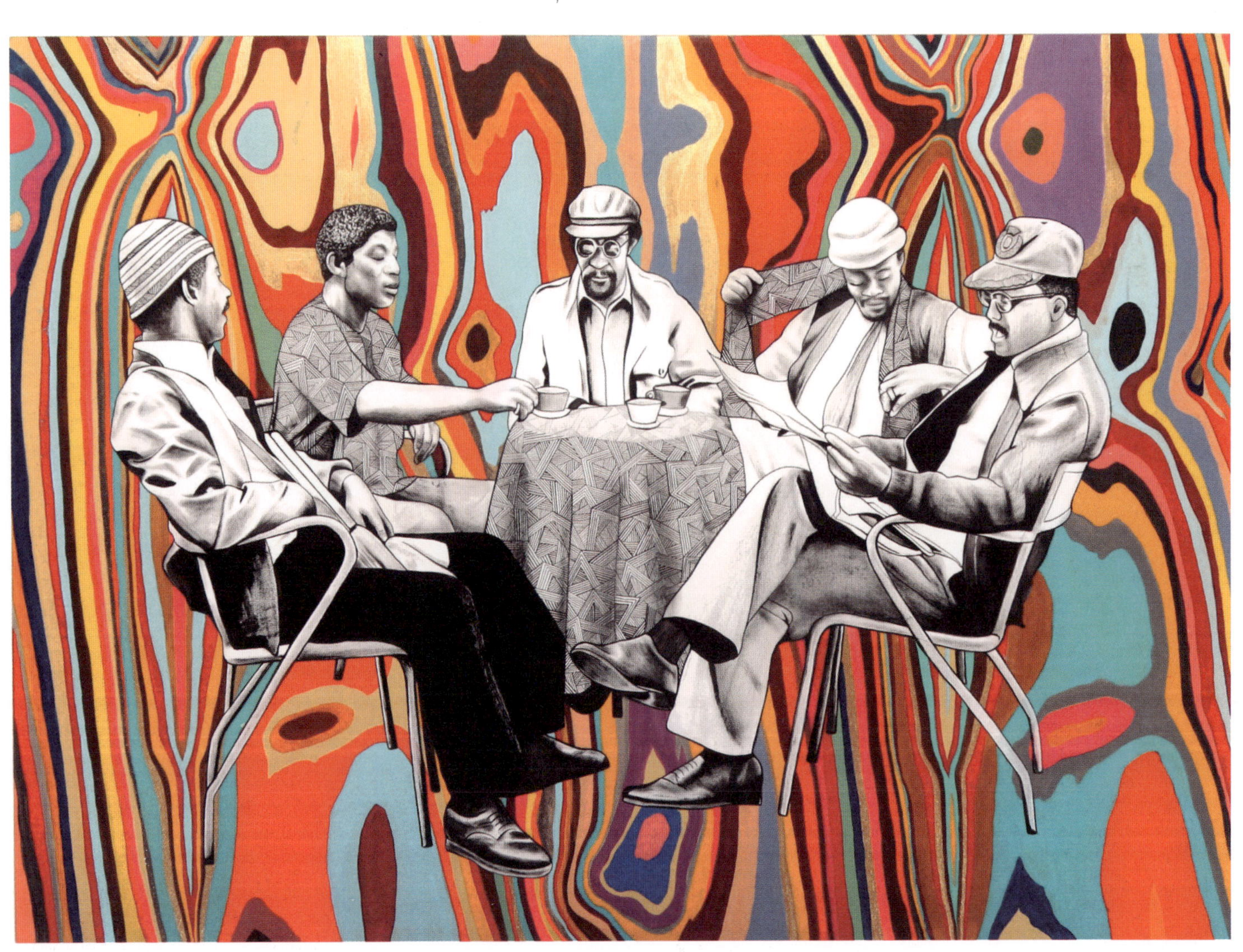

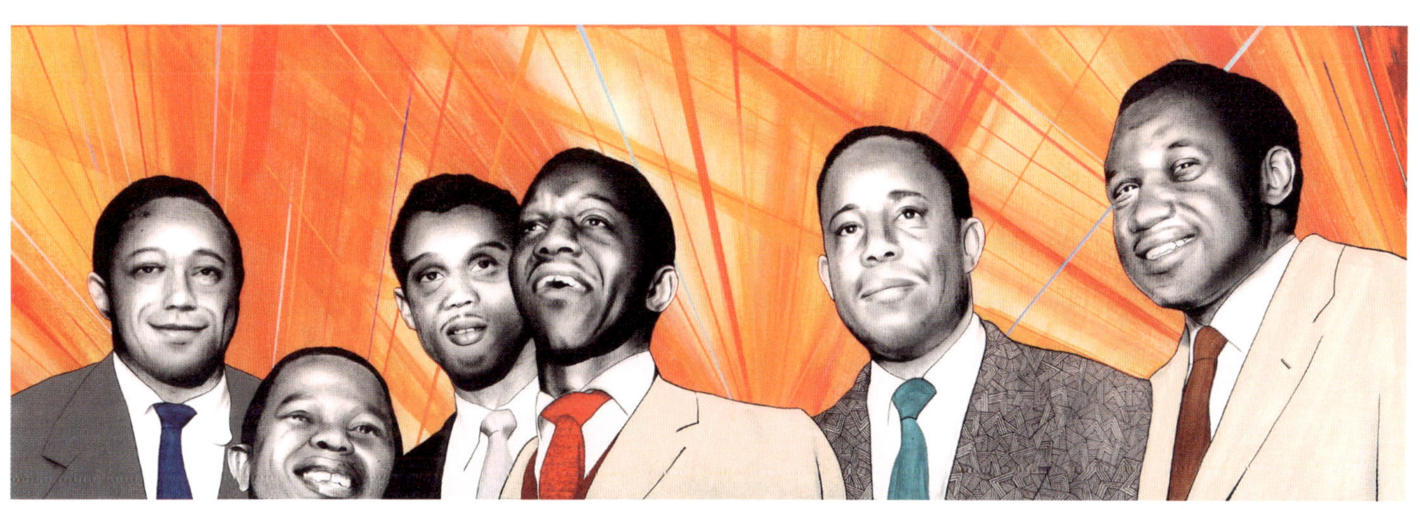

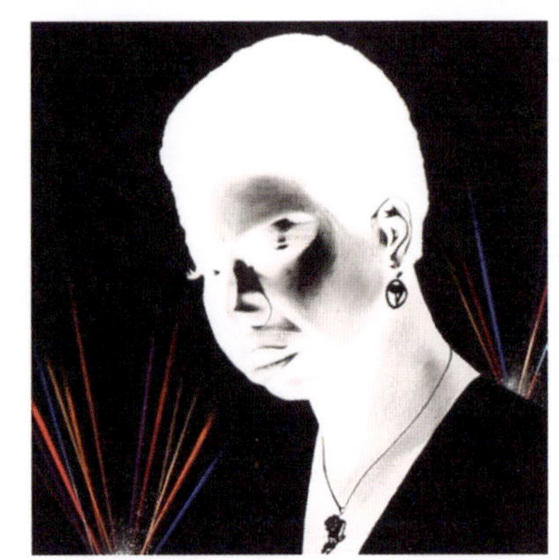

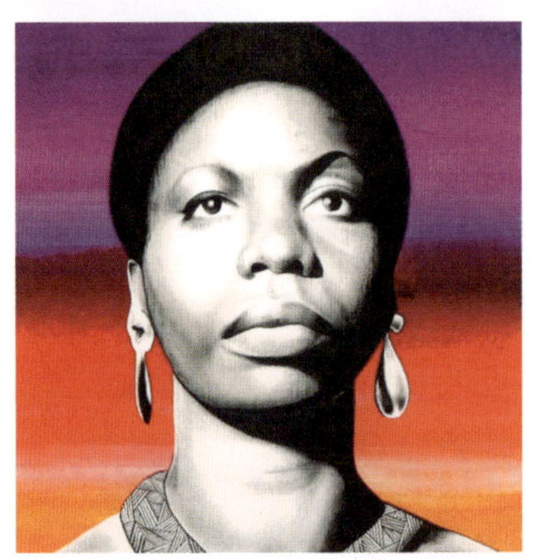

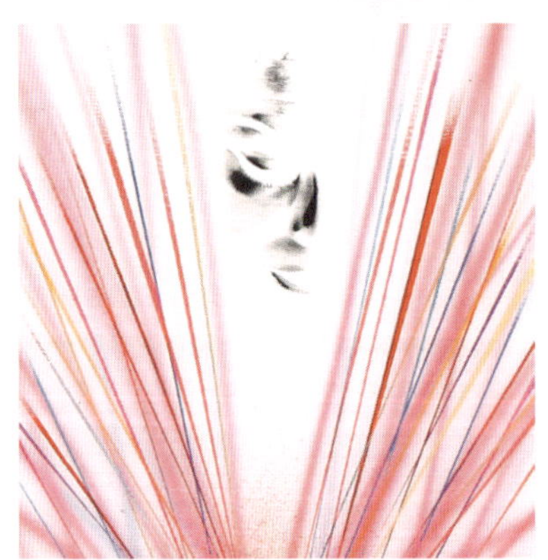

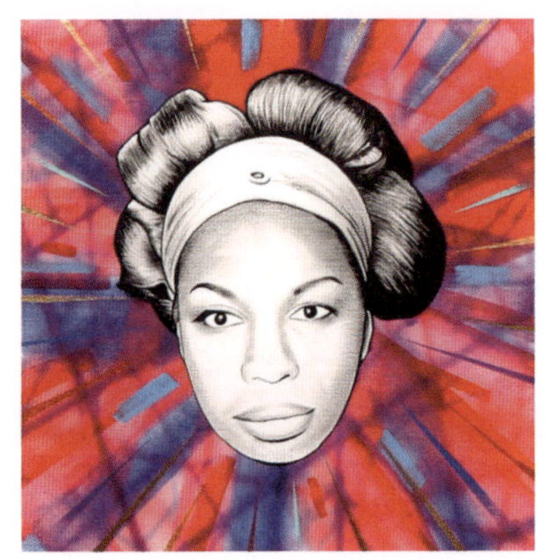

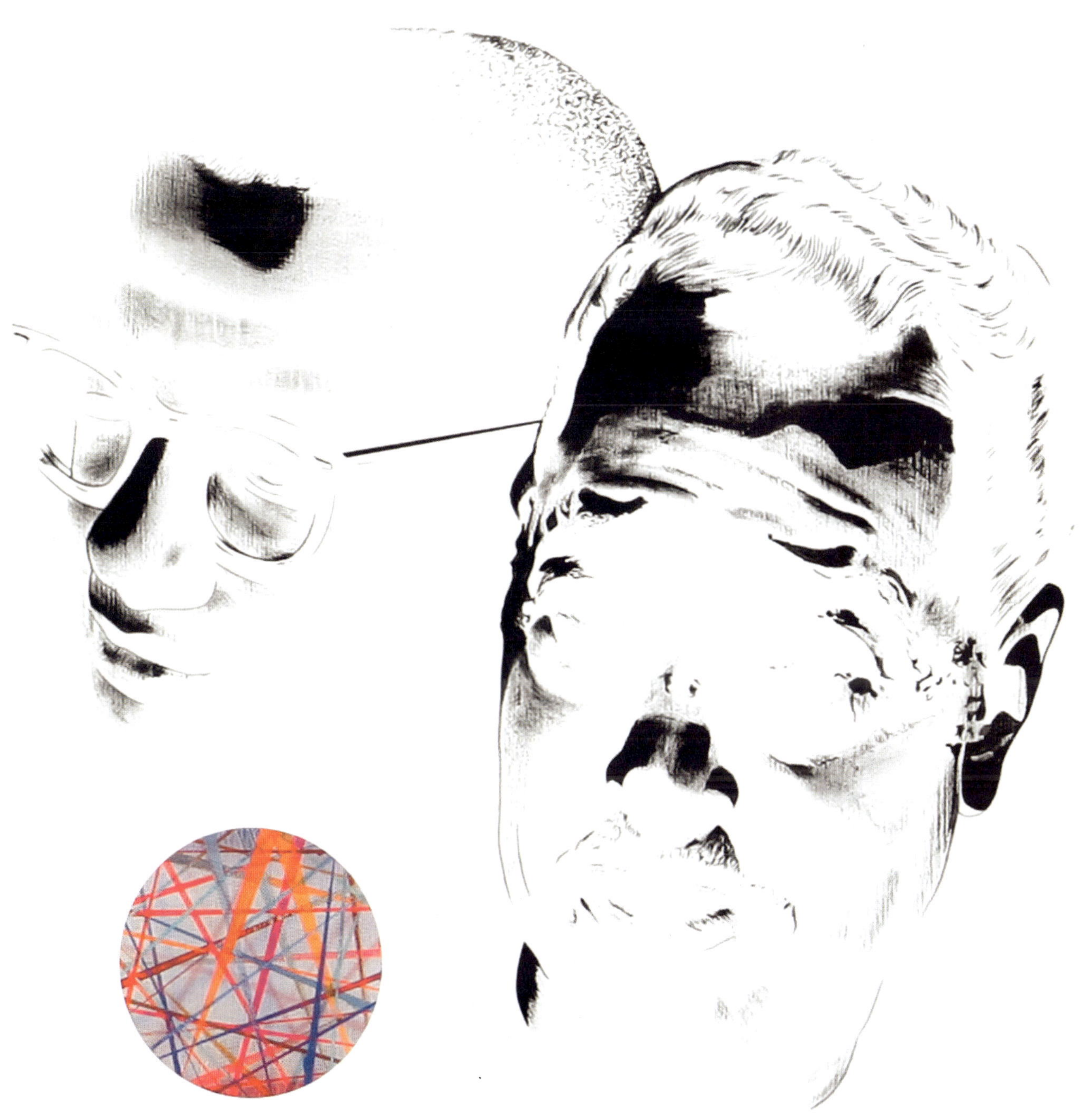

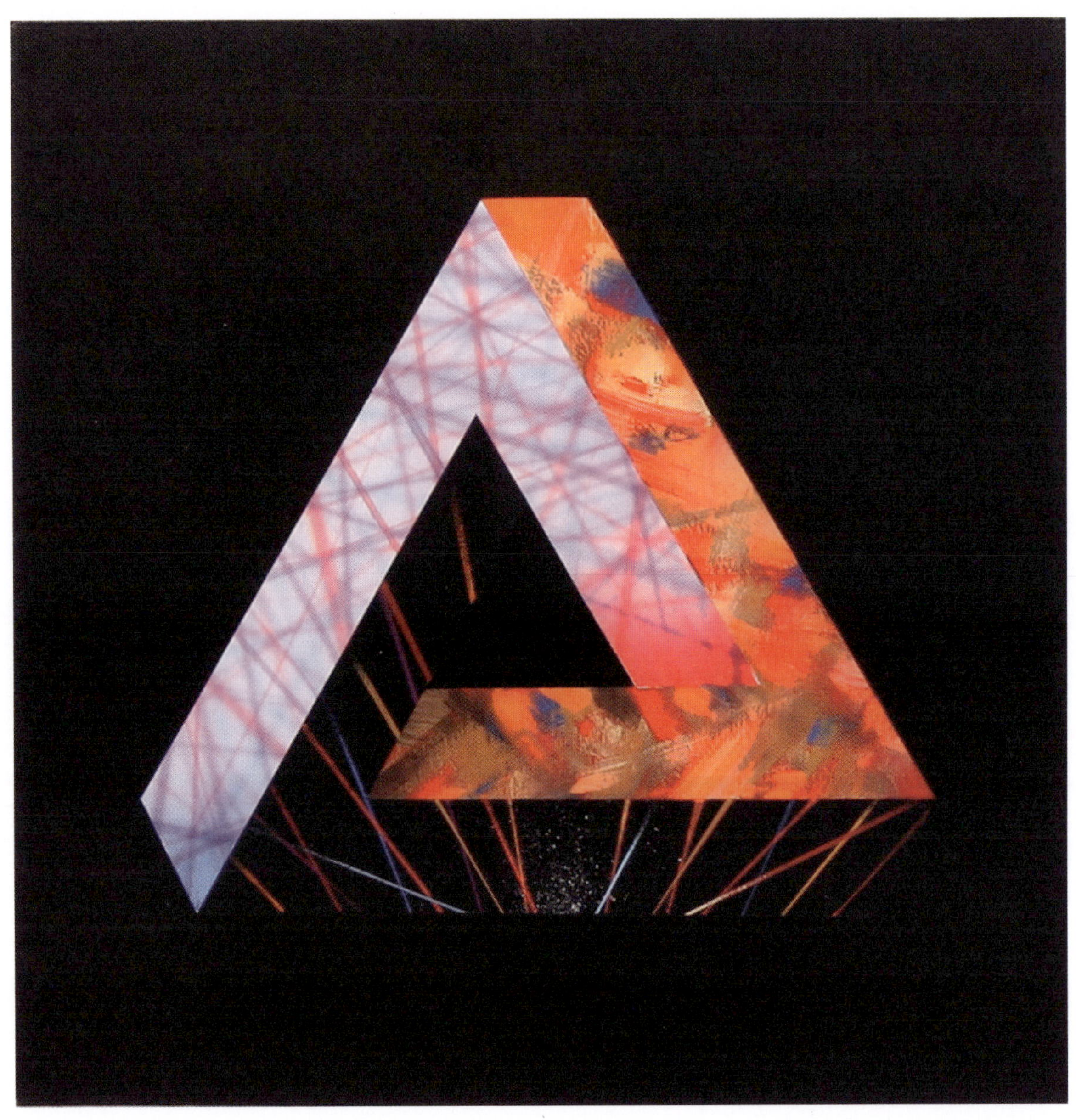

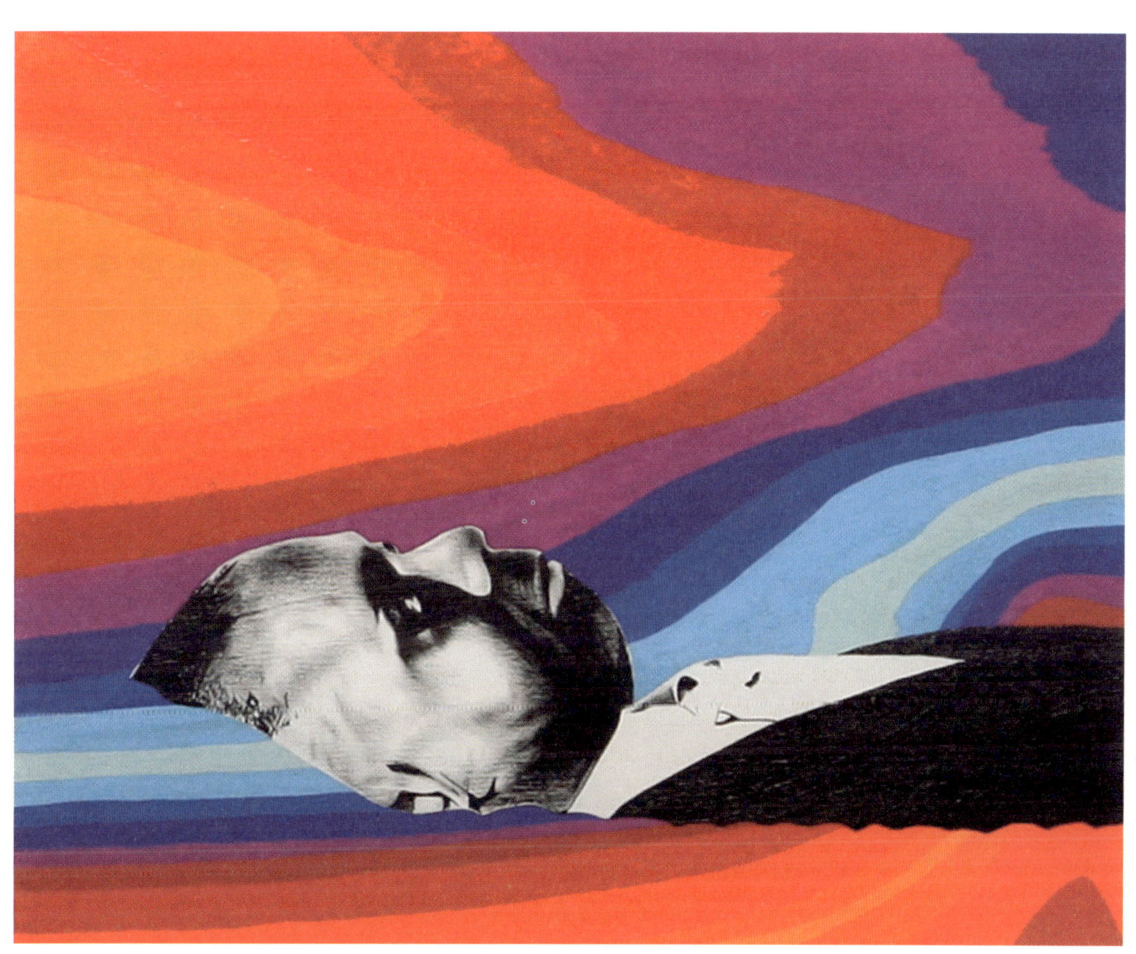

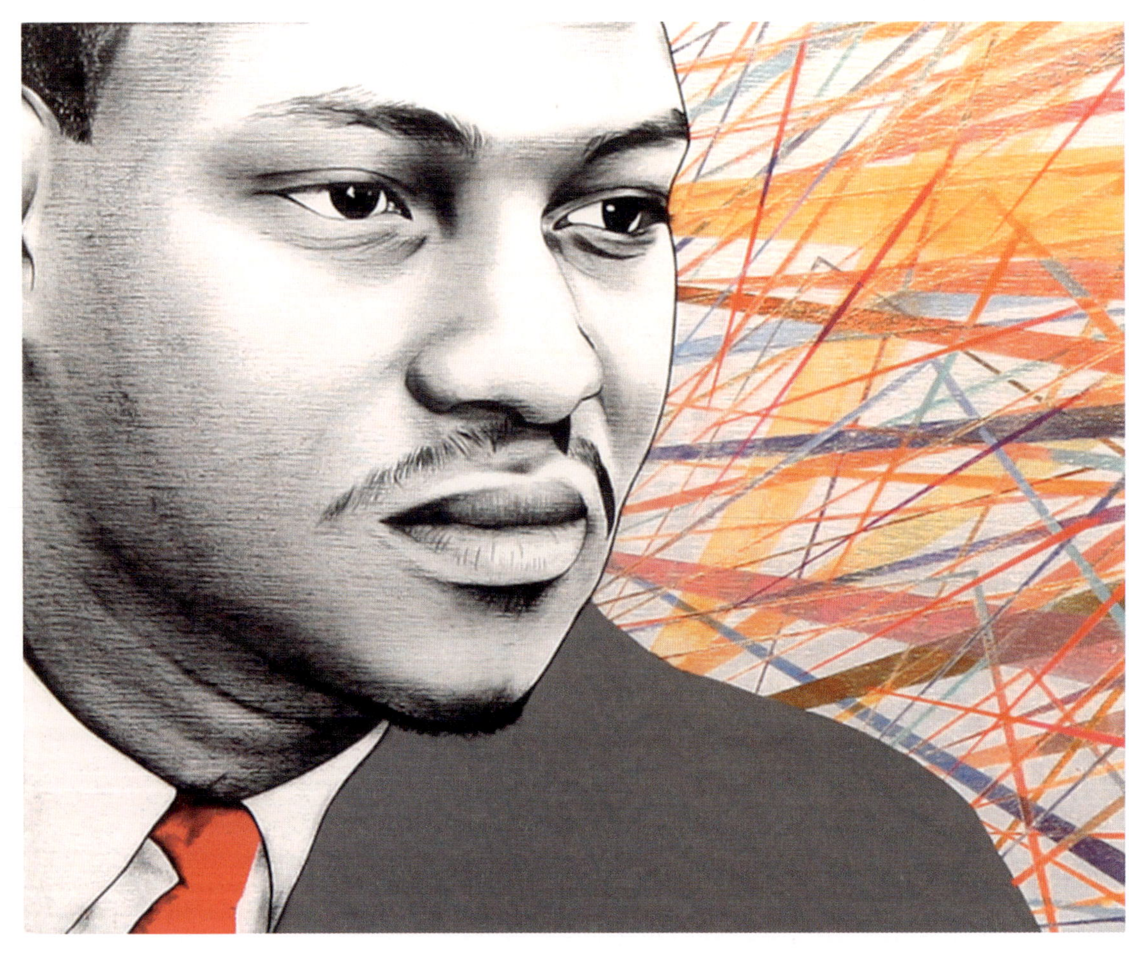

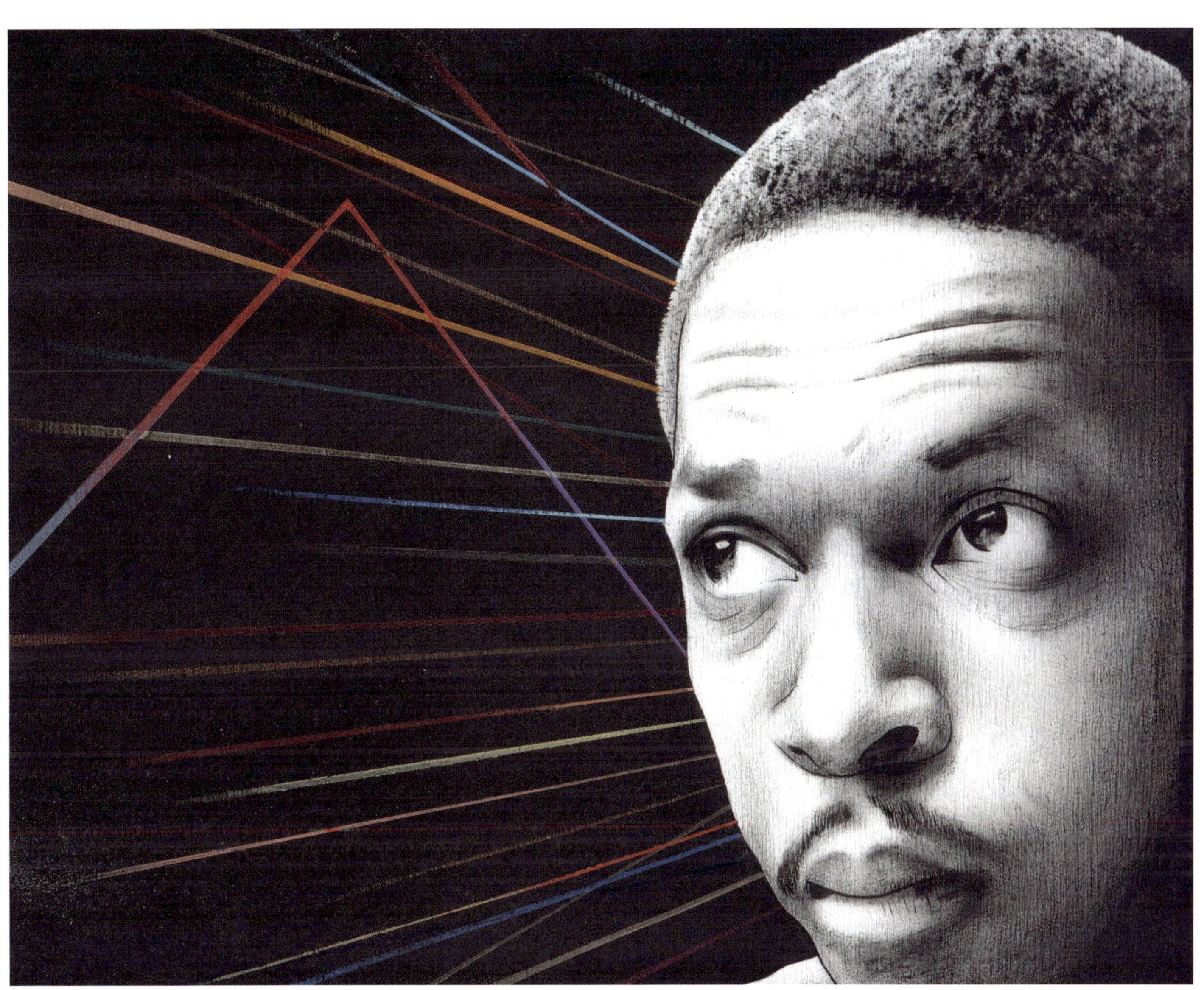

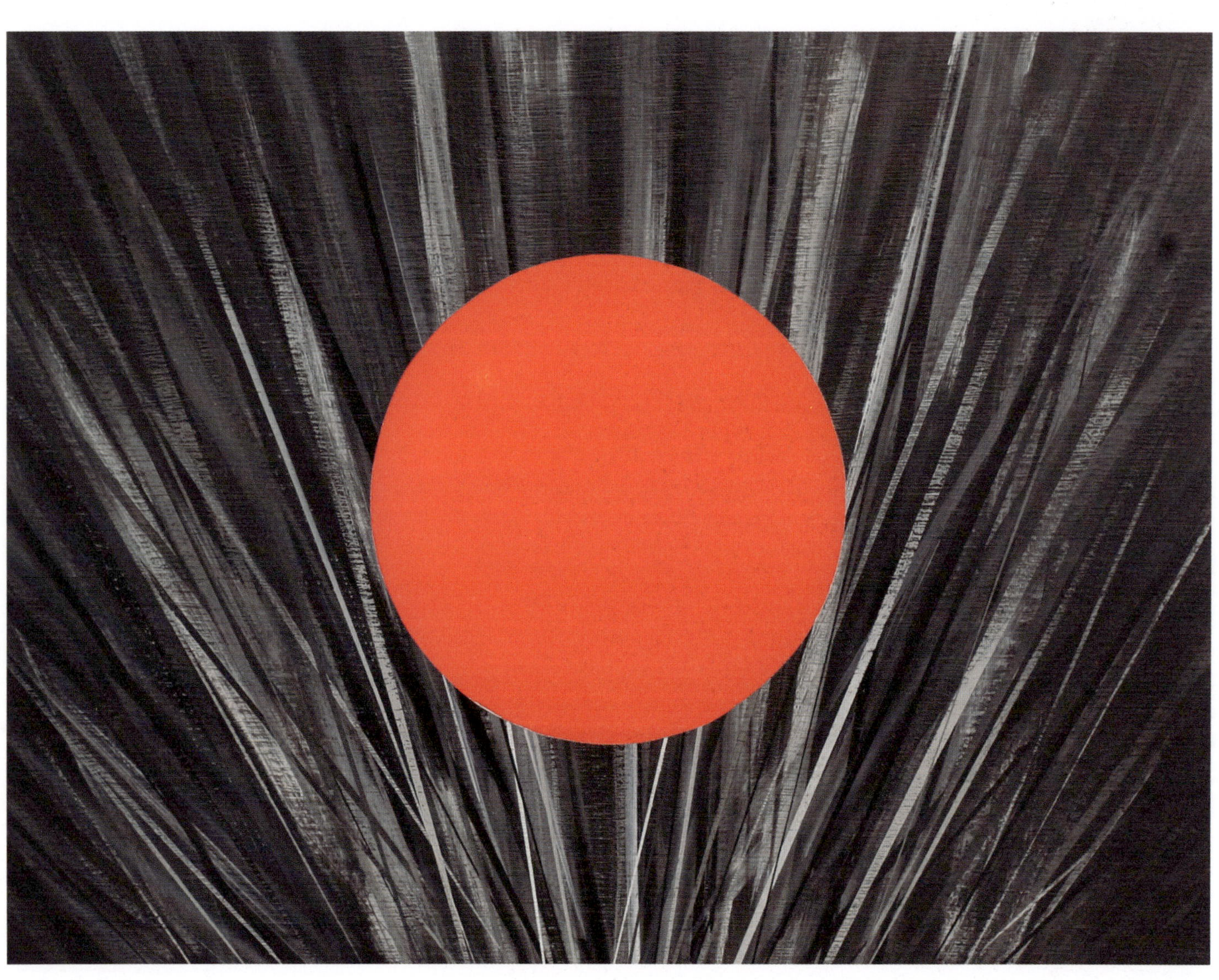

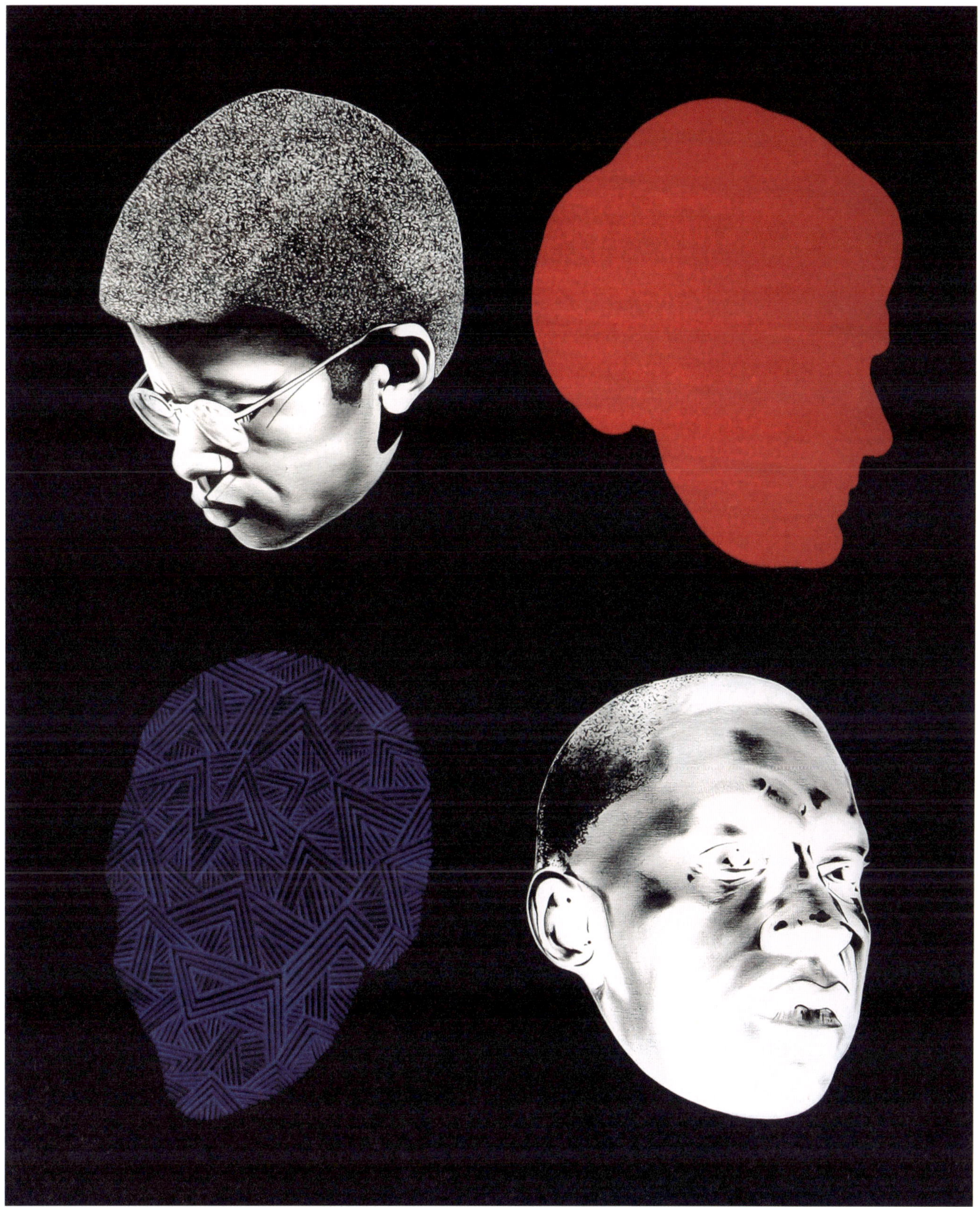

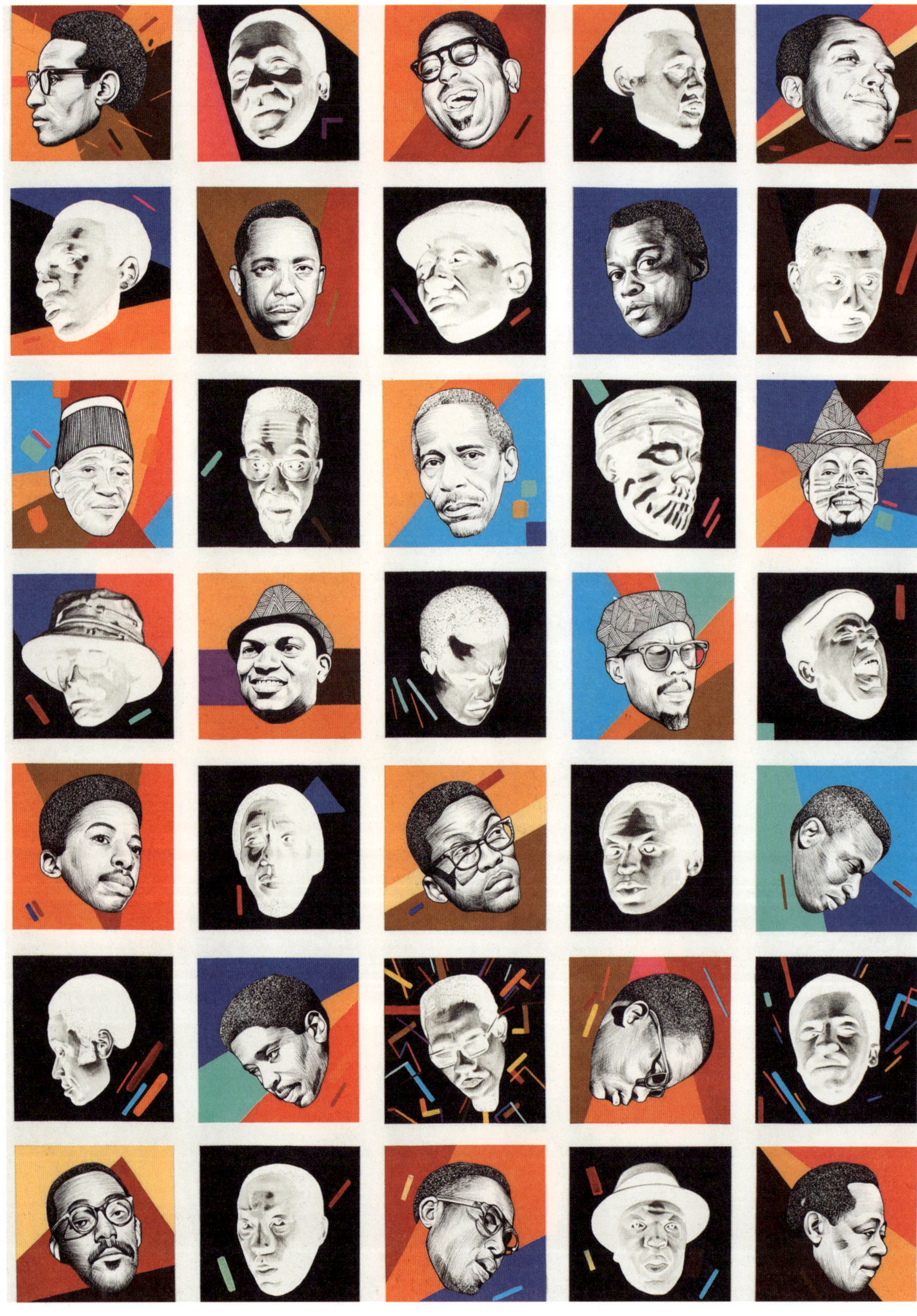

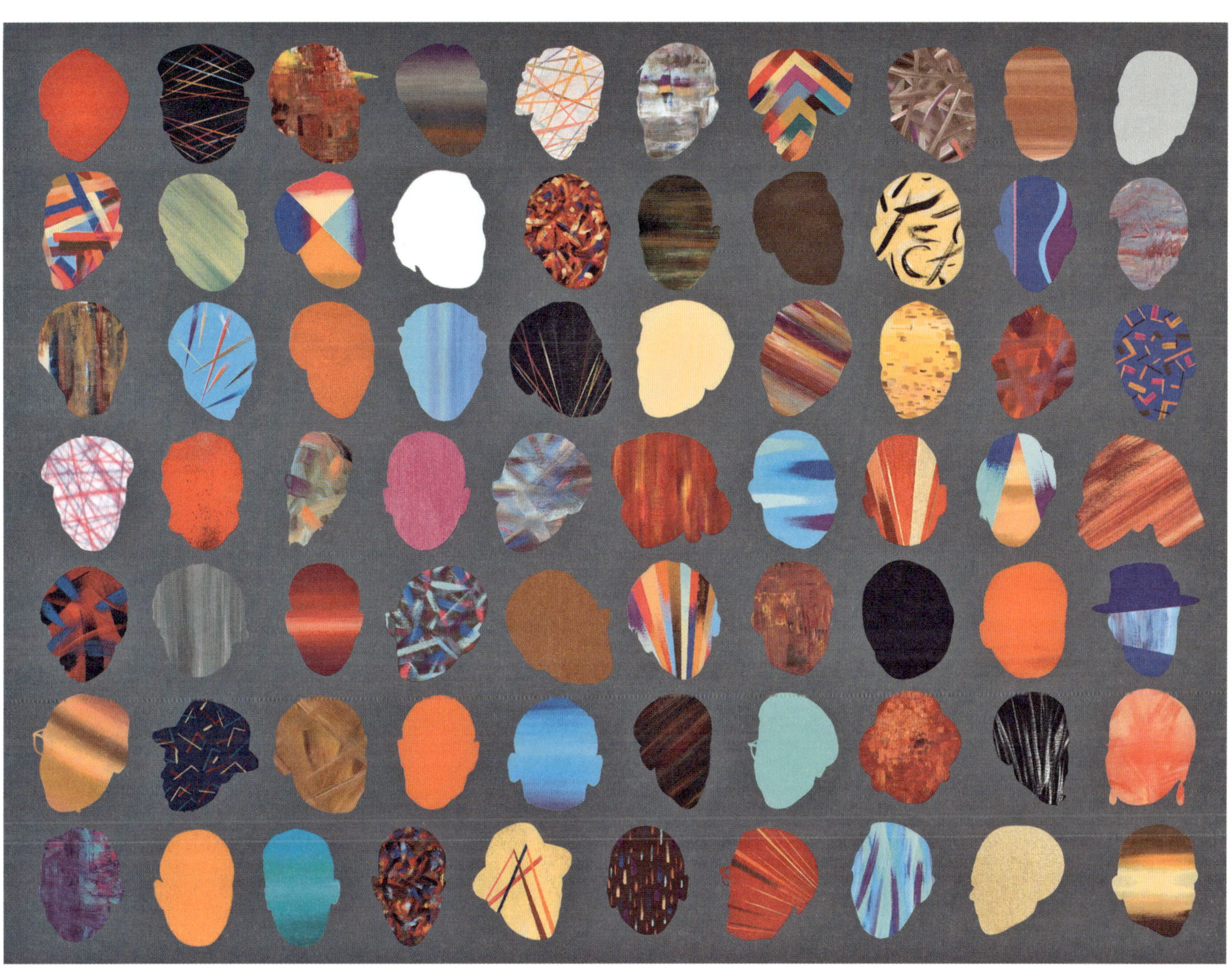

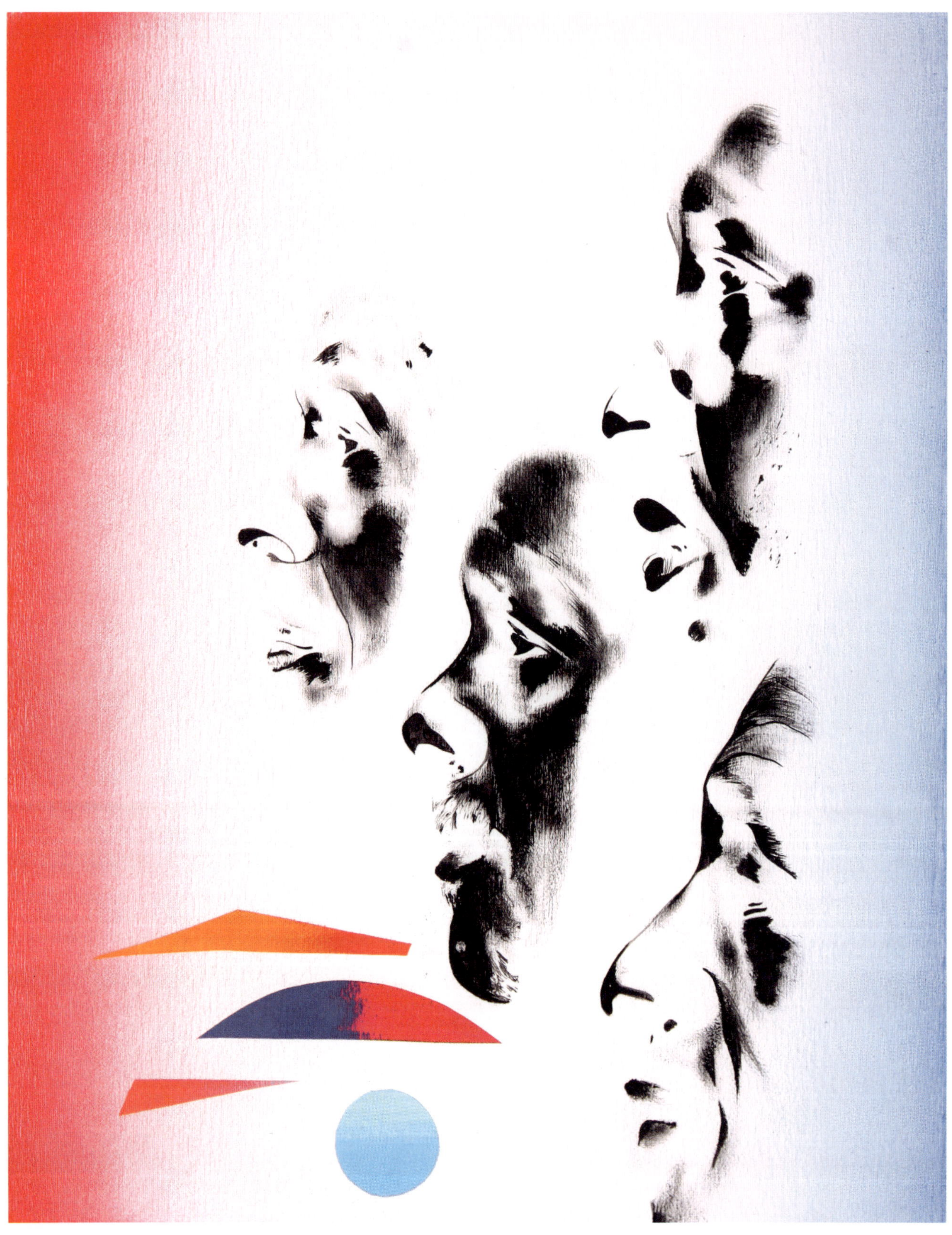

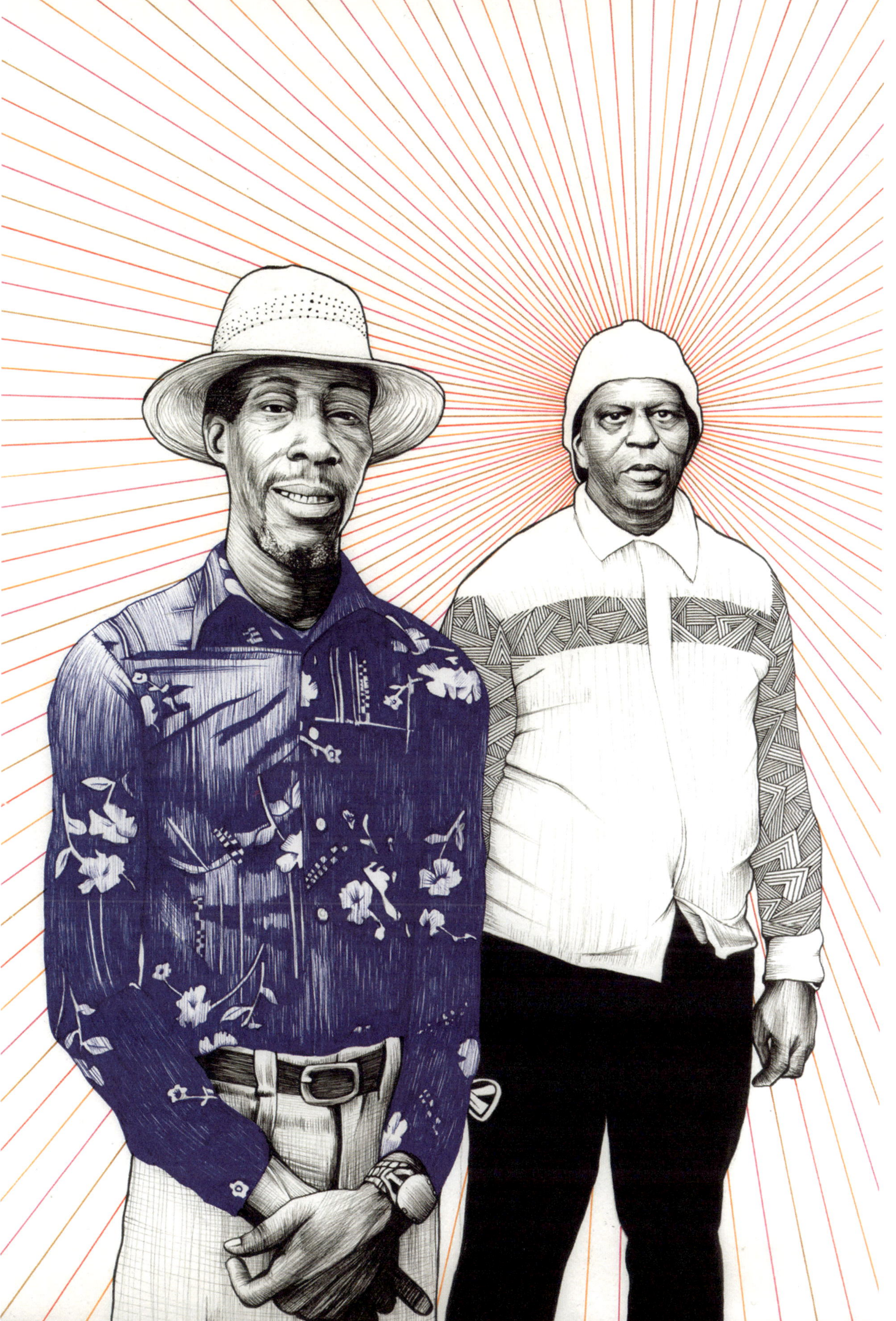

LIST OF WORKS

| 50 / 51 | ***THE FATHER, THE SON AND THE HOLY SPIRIT*** (Pharoah Sanders, John Coltrane, Albert Ayler), 2010, ink on paper, 22" x 12" |

50 / 51   ***THE FATHER, THE SON AND THE HOLY SPIRIT*** (Pharoah Sanders, John Coltrane, Albert Ayler), 2010, ink on paper, 22" x 12"

52   ***BILL EVANS TRIO***, 2011, ink on paper, 12" x 12"

53   ***UNTITLED*** (Heads Nº 16), 2013, ink and gouache on paper, 17" x 14"

54   ***THE GATHERING*** (Dizzy, Mary Lou Williams, Hank Jones, Tadd Dameron, Milt Orent), 2012, acrylic on panel, 30" x 24"

55   ***NIGHT IN NIGHT OUT*** (Chet Baker), 2011, acrylic on panel, 10" x 8"

56   ***COOL BREEZE*** (Chet Baker), 2011, Collaboration with Sadie Barnette, ink and gouache on paper, 11" x 14"

57   ***UNTITLED*** (Herbie Hancock), 2011, Collaboration with Sadie Barnette, ink and gouache on paper, 10" x 8"

58   ***UNTITLED*** (Billie Holiday), 2011, Collaboration with Sadie Barnette, ink and spray paint on paper, 14" x 11"

59   ***UNTITLED*** (Herbie Hancock), 2011, Collaboration with Sadie Barnette, ink and spray paint on paper, 9" x 12"

60   ***VENDÔME*** (Modern Jazz Quartet), 2012, ink and gouache on paper, 30" x 22"

61   ***FAR CRY II*** (Eric Dolphy), 2014, ink and gouache on paper, 22" x 15"

62   ***I WONDER*** (Lucille & Louis Armstrong), 2012, ink and acrylic on paper, 30" x 22"

63   ***UNTITLED*** (Louis Armstrong), 2011, ink and acrylic on paper, 9" x 12"

64   ***DAAHOUD*** (Max Roach & Clifford Brown), 2012, gouache and ink on paper, 15" x 22"

65   ***A JOYFUL NOISE*** (Sun Ra), 2013, acrylic and gouache on panel, 44" x 48"

66   ***UNTITLED*** (Joe Pass), 2012, acrylic on panel, 10" x 10"

67   ***UNTITLED*** (John Coltrane), 2009, ink on paper, 7" x 5"

68   ***UNTITLED*** (Nat King Cole & Earl Hines), 2010, ink on paper, 10" x 8"

69   ***BLACK KEYS*** (Heads Nº 9), 2011, ink on paper, 10" x 8"

70   ***QUARTETS THAT NEVER WERE VOL.1*** (Art Blakey, Albert Ayler, Charles Mingus, Mary Lou Williams), 2012, ink and gouache on paper, 9" x 12"

71   ***TWIN STARS OF THENCE***, 2010, acrylic on panel, 10" x 8"

72   ***BLUE MONK IN EUROPE*** (Thelonious Monk), 2010, ink and acrylic on paper, 9" x 12"

73   ***POINT OF DEPARTURE*** (Andrew Hill), 2010, acrylic on panel, 10" x 8"

74   ***COMPOSITION Nº 1*** (Anthony Braxton), 2010, ink and acrylic on paper, 13" x 17"

75   ***THIS IS OUR MUSIC VOL.1*** (Ornette Coleman Quartet), 2013, acrylic on panel, 8" x 10"

76   ***IN YOUR OWN SWEET WAY*** (Dave Brubeck), 2012, ink and gouache on paper, 9" x 12"

77   ***UNTITLED*** (Sonny Stitt), 2012, ink on paper, 14" x 11"

78   ***VARIATIONS II*** (Murray, Ayler, Peacock), 2014, acrylic, spray paint and gouache on panel, 24" x 18"

79   ***BETWEEN TWO WORLDS*** (Heads Nº 18 / Marshall Allen & Sun Ra), 2013, acrylic and gouache on panel, 10" x 8"

80   ***FOLKUS*** (Art Ensemble Of Chicago), 2013, acrylic on panel, 22.5" x 18.5"

81   ***MAYREH*** (Horace Silver, Pee Wee, Doug Watkins, Art Blakey, Lou Donaldson, Clifford Brown), 2013, acrylic and gouache on panel, 35" x 12"

82   ***FOUR WOMEN*** (Nina Simone), 2013, acrylic and gouache on panel, 4 pieces 8" x 8" each

83   ***SOMETHING TO LIVE FOR*** (Billy Strayhorn And Duke Ellington), 2013, acrylic and gouache on panel, 12" x 12"

84   ***TRIO OF DOOM***, 2013, acrylic and gouache on panel, 10" x 10"

85   ***WHEN IT'S SLEEPY TIME DOWN SOUTH*** (Louis Armstrong), 2013, acrylic and gouache on panel, 10" x 8"

86   ***SEARCH FOR PEACE*** (Mccoy Tyner), 2013, acrylic and gouache on panel, 10" x 8"

87   ***UNTITLED*** (John Coltrane), 2012, acrylic and gouache on panel, 10" x 8"

88   ***IF YOU CAME FROM NOWHERE HERE*** 2014, acrylic and gouache on panel, 18" x 14"

89   ***POLITE BLUE SYMMETRY*** (Heads Nº 22 / Andrew Hill, Gary Peacock, John Coltrane, Art Blakey), 2013, acrylic on panel, 20" x 24"

90   ***QUINTETS***, 2013, gouache and ink on paper, 22" x 30"

91   ***UNTITLED*** (Heads Nº 25), 2013, acrylic and gouache on panel, 48" x 36"

92   ***ONE NEVER KNOWS*** (Modern Jazz Quartet), 2013, acrylic and gouache on panel, 8" x 10"

93   ***OTHER SIDE OF THE...*** (John Gilmore And Sun Ra), 2010, ink on paper, 13" x 17"

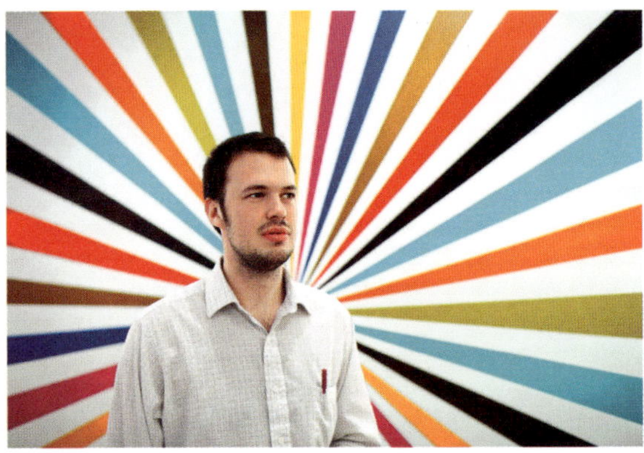

Inquiries should be addressed to:
Paper Museum Press
220 Clement Street
San Francisco, CA 94118
www.paper-museum.net
phone 415.386.7275
fax 415.386.7272

Published in Association with Gingko Press:
1321 Fifth Street
Berkeley, CA 94710 - USA
www.gingkopress.com

Printed in China
ISBN 978-0-9788739-8-1

Designed by Ian Johnson

Photography by Ando Caulfield, Ken Goto, Darrell Stein and Randy Dodson

www.ianmjohnson.com
www.parklifestore.com